KURT VONNEGUT, JR.
is a writer of driving energy, rich comic invention, and sheer exuberance. . . . He is a deeply
humane and very human writer whose six novels
have gained the admiration of countless younger
(and older) readers in recent years.

In *Kurt Vonnegut*, Peter J. Reed brings out both
the fantastic variety and the underlying coherence of the world of Vonnegut's imagination.

Kurt Vonnegut is the first volume in an exciting new series of critical appreciations called
WRITERS FOR THE SEVENTIES.

KURT
VONNEGUT, JR.

by

Peter J. Reed

University of Minnesota

WARNER
PAPERBACK
LIBRARY

A Warner Communications Company

WARNER PAPERBACK LIBRARY EDITION
First Printing: September, 1972
Second Printing: March, 1974

Copyright © 1972 by Warner Books, Inc.
All rights reserved.

*Warner Paperback Library is a division of Warner Books, Inc.
75 Rockefeller Plaza, New York, N.Y. 10019*

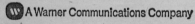 A Warner Communications Company

Printed in the United States of America

To the Memory of

James W. Hall

(1916–1971)

Acknowledgments

Grateful acknowledgment is made to Dell Publishing Company, Inc., for permission to quote throughout this book:

from *Player Piano* by Kurt Vonnegut, Jr. Copyright 1952 by Kurt Vonnegut, Jr. A Seymour Lawrence Book/ Delacorte Press. Reprinted by permission of the publisher.

from *The Sirens of Titan* by Kurt Vonnegut, Jr. Copyright © 1959 by Kurt Vonnegut, Jr. A Seymour Lawrence Book/Delacorte Press. Reprinted by permission of the publisher.

from *Mother Night* by Kurt Vonnegut, Jr. Copyright © 1961, 1966 by Kurt Vonnegut, Jr. A Seymour Lawrence Book/Delacorte Press. Reprinted by permission of the publisher.

from *Cat's Cradle* by Kurt Vonnegut, Jr. Copyright © 1963 by Kurt Vonnegut, Jr. A Seymour Lawrence Book/Delacorte Press. Reprinted by permission of the publisher.

from *God Bless You, Mr. Rosewater* by Kurt Vonnegut, Jr. Copyright © 1965 by Kurt Vonnegut, Jr. A Seymour Lawrence Book/Delacorte Press. Reprinted by permission of the publisher.

from *Slaughterhouse-Five* by Kurt Vonnegut, Jr. Copyright © 1969 by Kurt Vonnegut, Jr. A Seymour Lawrence Book/Delacorte Press. Reprinted by permission of the publisher.

In addition, the author would like to thank Harcourt Brace Jovanovich, Inc., for permission to quote from "Burnt Norton" by T. S. Eliot (*The Complete Poems and Plays of T. S. Eliot*); and Doubleday & Company, Inc., for permission to quote from "The Waking" by Theodore Roethke (*The Collected Poems of Theodore Roethke*).

Foreword

Kurt Vonnegut, Jr.: A Writer for the Seventies

Kurt Vonnegut, Jr., by Peter J. Reed, is the first volume in a series of four critical appreciations under the collective title, "Writers for the Seventies." Other books in this series are *Richard Brautigan,* by Terence Malley; *Hermann Hesse,* by Edwin F. Casebeer; and *J.R.R. Tolkien,* by Robley Evans. The intention of these studies is to provide clear and balanced discussions of the main themes and techniques of the four authors in question. In each case, the critic has avoided excessively technical, academic terminology. In general, the four critics have addressed their subjects directly or even personally, without the sort of detachment that makes so many critical studies seem remote. Hopefully, the volumes

11

in the Writers for the Seventies series will serve as good introductions to the four authors under discussion, for readers only slightly familiar with their books, while offering fresh insights for those who have already read the major works of Vonnegut, Brautigan, Hesse, and Tolkien.

A second—less direct—intention of the Writers for the Seventies series is to help, in a small way, to bridge that large and apparently increasing gap between the high school and college age readers of today and their parents and/or teachers. Each of the critics involved in this project is a youngish professor at an American college. All four are in their thirties: old enough to have had their graduate training in what seems already, only ten or twelve years later, a time of relatively settled, traditional standards; young enough to feel the impact of today's counter culture and to be aware of their students' insistence on "relevance" in literature. In each volume, the emphasis is on critical *appreciation;* in each case, the critic tries to arrive at qualitative judgments about his author's achievement and to define the value of this author for readers of all ages.

But why these four authors in particular? Why Vonnegut, Brautigan, Hesse, and Tolkien? Early in his book, *Future Shock*, Alvin Toffler asserts that "Writers have a harder and harder time keeping up with reality."* And, of course, it is possible that the "reality" captured by these four writers will soon cease to hold the attention of readers, that each of the four will soon be seen as someone who had a certain vogue in the late 1960's and early 1970's and then faded off the bookstore racks and out of the minds of readers. This is possible, but not, I think, probable. Despite the vagaries of taste and popularity, the strange chemistry that makes today's best-seller next year's remainder item, it seems likely that all four authors focused upon in the Writers for the Seventies series will continue to hold the attention of American readers, particularly younger readers of high school and college ages.

---

*New York: Bantam Books, 1971, p. 5.

Needless to say, the four authors are very different: Hesse, the Swiss pacifist, deep in Eastern religions and Jungian psychology; Tolkien, the Cambridge don, absorbed in medieval literature and philology; Vonnegut, the former PR man turned satirist of an increasingly dehumanized America; Brautigan, that transitional figure between the Beat Generation and the Hippies, concerned with a gentle world of trout fishing and green growing things. . . . Indeed, if we were to imagine the four of them in some Paradise of Authors (or—that favorite test-question situation—cast up together on a desert island), we might very well decide that they would have little to say to each other, about their works, about their interests.

Yet, for all their differences, there are some important common denominators running through the works of Hesse, Tolkien, Vonnegut, and Brautigan. Perhaps outlining a few of these will partly explain why all four writers began to attract large audiences in the United States at approximately the same time. First of all, speaking broadly, all four can be described as fantasy-writers. Whether through interior fantasies (like *Steppenwolf* and *In Watermelon Sugar*) or through exterior fantasies (like *The Lord of the Rings* and *The Sirens of Titan*)— all four authors use fantasy to comment on reality. Of course, any successful fantasy (from fairytale to science fiction) comments in some way or other on ordinary reality. But our four authors have all, in their very different ways, been able to give their fantasies the sort of internal coherence, plausibility, and substance that enable their readers to suspend disbelief and accept what Coleridge called the "poetic truth" behind fantasy.

In common with virtually every significant writer of the last half-century, the reality behind their fantasies is pretty grim. In all four authors, a war—World War I or World War II—serves as either implicit or explicit background. The appalling catastrophe of the First World War, the slaughter of an entire generation of young men, seems always just beneath the surface of Hesse's major works; in Tolkien, the vast carnage of World War II paralleled exactly the composition of his own version of

13

an ultimate struggle between forces of light and darkness; the Second World War has had the most direct influence on Vonnegut, who was in the war, a POW and a miraculous survivor of the hideous fire-bombing of Dresden; for Brautigan, the youngest of the four authors, World War II is coincident with his earliest conscious memories, and stands ironically as a time of coherence, when things were easier to understand than they could ever be again.

All four authors would surely agree with the "moral" of Vonnegut's *Mother Night*: "We are what we pretend to be, so we must be careful about what we pretend to be." In all four, this bare statement is developed in rich, complex terms. All four are ultimately concerned with self-definition, with the problem of a person's realizing his full humanity (or, in Tolkien's case, I suppose we must also say his full hobbithood). In all four, self-fulfillment is threatened by an essentially dehumanized and dehumanizing world: Hesse's world of vulgar materialism, Tolkien's world in which Sauron aspires to enslave the spirits of all living creatures, Vonnegut's world in which machines often threaten to replace humanity, Brautigan's world of dropouts from a society without sustaining values.

Finally—and perhaps the most important thing Hesse, Tolkien, Vonnegut, and Brautigan have in common—all four authors share an affirmative sense of the possibilities of the human spirit. Without denying the pitfalls that surround their characters, without settling for facile optimism, all four of these Writers for the Seventies show us in their works that there are still things a person can do, that there are still values to be found by looking around oneself and (even more important) by looking *within* oneself. In this time of disillusionment and danger, we need writers like Hesse, Tolkien, Vonnegut, and Brautigan—to remind us that Joy is still possible, to teach us (in Hesse's phrase) how to hear the laughter of the Immortals.

Peter J. Reed's *Kurt Vonnegut, Jr.*, focuses on the six novels written by Vonnegut between 1952 and 1969, between, that is to say, a time of witch hunts and conformity and a time of bitter protest, repression, disillusionment. In his discussions of Vonnegut's novels, Reed brings out not only the characteristic themes emerging from the books but also the many fictional techniques by which Vonnegut conveys his themes. As a result, we get a sense of the rich bounty of the world of Vonnegut's imagination—the energy, the comic invention, the sheer exuberance.

As Reed says, Vonnegut is an author who compels our affection as well as our admiration. For all the tough-minded skepticism, satiric anger, and deep pessimism in his novels, we feel in reading Vonnegut that behind the books stands a truly compassionate and gentle man, a very human person as well as a very humane one. We are not in the least surprised to learn, in *Slaughterhouse-Five*, that Lot's wife is one of Vonnegut's favorite characters; he loves her, he says, because "it was so human" for her to insist on looking back on Sodom and Gomorrah.

Even if Vonnegut holds to his present declared intention to write no more novels, I believe that he will continue to attract readers, and that his reputation as a significant writer will continue to increase. For one thing, two of his works—*Slaughterhouse-Five* and the play, *Happy Birthday, Wanda June*—have recently been made into films (in addition, another novel, *Player Piano,* is said to be in movie-production). And hopefully these film versions will send people to the books, as the books have sent people to the films. But even apart from that consideration, I think that Vonnegut's novels will continue to live (especially with younger readers) because his combination of idealism and skepticism, of nostalgia for the past that might have been and awareness of the present that all-too-painfully *is* (as well as of the grim future that seems likely, if not inevitable), makes such obvious and necessary sense.

Vonnegut is a modest writer, as his half-serious self-comparisons to the woefully unsuccessful science-fiction author, Kilgore Trout, suggest. Vonnegut would probably deny what I think are the most important qualities that

Peter Reed brings out about him: that Vonnegut is ultimately as *sane* and as *wise* as any writer of our time.

Vonnegut prefers to describe himself as a Kilgore Trout, as an old fart, as a pillar of salt, as a failure. But, then, Vonnegut also reminds us that he is "a very funny writer" too.

Terence Malley
Long Island University
Brooklyn, New York

Contents

Preface

One evening late in the Second World War, I stood in the garden of my home just outside London and watched the fading sky darkened with the black wings of hundreds of Lancasters and Halifaxes. Bombers were strewn across the sky, and after it was too dark to see them anymore the throb of their engines went on and on. It remains one of my most indelible memories. Others, registered equally deeply, come from earlier in the war: of the London Blitz, of dogfights in an always blue sky, of air-raid shelters, of being bombed out. And I remember that even as a boy, watching those British bombers wing in almost endless stream toward Hamburg, or Cologne, or perhaps even Dresden, I felt a mixture of satisfaction that we were "giving it back to 'em" and sympathy for those on whom that great aerial armada would rain terror, shock and death. There is no ambivalence in my feelings about the German bombing of Britain; there is still much in my thinking about the Allied mass bombings of German cities. So if there is any personal bias to declare which might influence what I have to say about Kurt Vonnegut's writing, that is it.

These wartime events, which left their mark on me and which are at the center of much of Vonnegut's thinking and writing, occurred before most of those who are largely responsible for his current popularity were born. That fact might be significant. It first suggests that Vonnegut's vision of the world, obviously shaped largely by events of the forties, has been presented in terms which somehow give it a particular appeal in the sixties and seventies. There could be a case for the universality of his fiction to be made from that. Secondly, it indicates that there are good reasons why Vonnegut could appeal to an audience older than the one usually credited with being almost solely responsible for his popularity. In fact, he does have plenty of fans among the "over thirties," even if often they were introduced to him by younger friends and relatives. Last, I have taken this rather paradoxical fact as a hint that, if indeed Vonnegut's chief following is among those born after the war, it would be a mistake for me, who can remember that war, to try to explain why.

Much of the published commentary on Kurt Vonnegut explores the phenomenon of his late-blooming, fast-growing popularity, particularly among young readers. Beyond a doubt that makes an interesting topic—so interesting, in fact, that it has led some writers, even reviewers of specific books, away from serious consideration of the fiction itself into speculation on the nature of the following generated by it. My own shirt-cuff survey would indicate that Vonnegut is indeed widely popular among the late-teens early-twenties set, though for a wider variety of reasons than certain of the printed discussions of the subject suggest. Some in this audience seem to think he is a good writer, others to believe that he is a poor writer but therefore to be embraced as an appropriate voice for the counterculture. Some express the belief that he should be read for fun and above all not "institutionalized," while others will say that he is just the sort of writer college literature courses should include. I have attempted to look at how and why the novels work in their own right. I have sometimes placed particular emphasis upon contemporary social significance, since the fiction often demands it, and I have occasionally touched on the matter of "youth appeal" when it seems particularly appropriate, but my approach generally has been to discuss what seem to be the more important ideas and techniques in the novels, and how effectively they are rendered. I would hope this approach might help to explain the current popularity of Vonnegut while also permitting some evaluation of his work on a more solid basis than vogue.

Professional literary people seem to be the most divided over Vonnegut. Reviewers and critics contradict each other vigorously in their assessments. To illustrate, let me offer two of the more extensive and thoughtful pieces which take opposing positions—though they do not represent the extremes. Writing in *Esquire*, Leslie Fiedler views Vonnegut as a transitional or bridging figure between High Art and Pop, between Modernism and Post-Modernism, between the serious Art Novel and the New Romantic fantasy.[1] Fiedler points to the Western as the original American Pop, "that tale of male companions, red and white, in flight from women and in quest of the absolute wilderness, . . ." which exists from James Fennimore Cooper to the present and to which the American writer returns "to indulge not his own exclusive fantasies of alienation and closeness, but the dreams he shares with everyone else." Out of this Pop-fantasy tradition arises the New Romanticism, "which prefers sentimentality to irony, passion to reason, vulgarity to subtlety." Vonnegut stands halfway between the emergent Pop forms, the New

---

[1] Leslie A. Fiedler, "The Divine Stupidity of Kurt Vonnegut," *Esquire*, LXXIV (September, 1970), 195–204.

Romanticism, and the Modernism fathered by Eliot. He remains personally ambivalent, divided between wanting to appeal to the Pop audience and his apparent desire to win respect as a "serious writer." But his writing "*does* belong to what we know again to be the mainstream of fiction; it is not the mainstream of High Art, however, but of myth and entertainment: a stream which was forced underground over the past several decades, but has now surfaced once more." Vonnegut reaches his best, Fiedler judges, when he uses science fiction as "a way of releasing his own sentimental-ironic view of a meaningless universe redeemed by love," as in *The Sirens of Titan* and *Cat's Cradle*.

Far less laudatory in his assessment of Vonnegut is Charles Thomas Samuels.[2] He concludes that Vonnegut "can tell us nothing worth knowing except what his rise itself indicates: ours is an age in which adolescent ridicule can become a mode of upward mobility." Like Fiedler, Samuels refers to Vonnegut as a "bridge," but of a different sort, one who gives adult readers belonging to "an age of skepticism and baffled hope" easy access to an age "of faith in any nostrum that bears the certifications of novelty and youth." He suggests that to appreciate Vonnegut one must be pre-convinced, already persuaded to his position and taken with his books in general to accept one like *Cat's Cradle*. In sum, Samuels finds Vonnegut a "bogus talent" whose novels lack structure, precision or serious thought and whose characters are "one-dimensional grotesques impersonating people." Vonnegut, he finds, "is a sententious old salt in ontological drag." As for the young, whose adoration of Vonnegut Fiedler finds an affirmation, they essentially like the novelist for the wrong reasons, partly because Vonnegut's own "spiritual age is late adolescence. . . ."

---

[2]Charles Thomas Samuels, "Age of Vonnegut," *The New Republic,* CLXIV, (June 12, 1971), 30-32.

The short stories have not been included for discussion, except for occasional mention in passing. In his second collection, *Welcome to the Monkey House* (1970), Vonnegut appears to dismiss the stories as hack work done to support the writing of novels. Some look like it; others do not. But most of what they say is said with amplification, and generally said better, in the novels. Besides, in a short study one has to draw the line. For these same reasons, the play, *Happy Birthday, Wanda June* (1971), has been excluded. The main chapters take the novels in turn, in order of their publication. Each chapter treats what seems to me most important in a particular novel's central action and character. I have also attempted to make each chapter focus upon the aspect of Vonnegut's techniques most apparent in that novel, so that the discussions combined give a cumulative overview of the development of thought and method in the fiction. At the beginning of every chapter appears a plot summary. I offer these summaries in the hope that they might make their chapters reasonably intelligible to the reader not familiar with all of Vonnegut's novels, or that they may helpfully refresh the memories of those who finished any given novel some time ago.

I have used Avon Books' Bard Editions of *Player Piano* and *Mother Night*, the new Dell editions of *The Sirens of Titan*, *Cat's Cradle* and *God Bless You, Mr. Rosewater*, and Dell's Delta Books edition of *Slaughterhouse-Five*, all of which first appeared in 1970. The page references throughout are to these editions.

Mimi Heubner, Maggie Nagan, Dorothy Loosbrock and Monta Hemsing gave patient and friendly assistance in preparing the manuscript. Fluffy Olson diligently compiled a sizable checklist of writings on and by Vonnegut. To my old friend Terry Malley go my thanks for his encouragement and understanding, and my congratulations on his ability to maintain his characteristic cheer through times of trial. I have attempted to acknowledge a profoundly felt debt in the dedication. My wife Margaret persuaded me to undertake this book and more than anyone helped me to finish it. Provided I qualify, perhaps I can express my thoughts in Kurt Vonnegut's words: "All writers' wives are beautiful."

I

The Nostalgic Future of Player Piano

The first of Kurt Vonnegut's novels, *Player Piano* (1952), ostensibly talks about the future. Its setting is the city of Ilium, New York, some years after "the Second Industrial Revolution." Yet for all its technological sophistication and social innovation, the America described in this book resembles the one we live in, and we quickly realize that what Vonnegut wants to tell us about is not so much the future as the present. For the future we are shown derives from the present we know through direct extension or exaggeration. Sometimes playfully, sometimes angrily, Vonnegut mocks and debunks his fictional society, but the target always remains the same—the society he saw around him as he wrote. This satire of contemporary America by projection to a frightening future is pervaded by a note of nostalgia. The protagonist, other characters, and even the author himself, seem to indulge the notion that, the present being grim and the future holding little promise, the past must somehow have been better. Throughout the novel there runs the feeling that the failings of the past cannot possibly have been so dreadful as the advances that have sought to eradicate them, and that the good things have been lost. The social satire, the contemporary relevance, the humor, and the touch of yearning combine in *Player Piano* with fast pace and plenty of action. The combination is not always comfortable, however. At times *Player Piano* is serious to the point of being solemn, elsewhere it can be breezily lampooning. Yet it is in part the tension between derision and humane concern which lends the novel strength.

Player Piano recounts events which take place at some undefined point in the future in the town of Ilium, New York—a locale returned to by Vonnegut in some subsequent stories. The action centers around Doctor Paul Proteus, the thirty-five year old manager of the Ilium Works. (It has been speculated that Ilium and the Ilium Works derive from Vonnegut's own experience at General Electric in Schenectady, New York.) The United States is portrayed as an even more dominating world power than at present, having won that position in a world war which also gave the machine dominance over man. In order to meet wartime production demands and to make up the drainage of manpower into the services, machines have replaced manual labor and computers have taken over most of the supervision of the machines. Hence the vast Ilium Works is staffed by a handful of men, and at one point we even see an entire shift leaving work in a solitary station wagon. "Democracy," we are told ironically, "owed its life to know-how" (p. 9). In that democracy, however, all the real power lies in the hands of the managers and engineers, through the National Industrial Planning Board. Even the President turns out to be a brainless actor. Most production is by machine; only a few "skilled" occupations, such as barbering and professional athletics, remain open to men with less than a Ph.D. Since even engineering Ph.D.s are in small demand, students are screened rigorously (by computers) and only a select minority finds employment.

Proteus and his elite staff live in a kind of super-suburb on the Works side of the river, leading a parody-of-suburbia life of country club, social-climbing wives, cocktail parties, and professional one-upmanship. Across the river lies Homestead, a township of prefabricated "ticky-tacky boxes" for the masses who are mostly former employees of the Ilium Works. These people are "provided for" through the benefits of the Second Industrial Revolution. They are given self-cleaning houses, complete with instant cookers, dishwashers and laundry machines, color TVs and picture windows. For employment they have three choices: the Army, the Reconstruction and Reclamation Corps, or various forms of self-employment ranging from bartender to pool-shark. The Army, incidentally, has no guns except when sent overseas. The Second Industrial Revolution brought a wave of rebellion and machine-smashing which has given the manager-engineers an obsessional fear of sabotage and has led to the outlawing of guns—except for plant guards. The R.R.C., known as the "Reeks and Wrecks," dabbles mainly in road repair. Obviously, the Homesteaders do not think kindly of the Works people, while the latter regard Homestead roughly as Orange County looks on Watts, with a mixture of condescension, contempt, and fear.

From the start Proteus appears vaguely discontented, in spite of his having the number one job and the number one social position in Ilium, and a wife who is number one in glamor, hostessing, and general woman-behind-the-manism. He is being considered for promotion to management of the Pittsburgh Works and is the hot favorite for the post, partly for his own reputation as a bright young man and partly because his father was "the nation's first National Industrial, Commercial, Communications, Foodstuffs and Resources Director, a position approached in importance only by the presidency of the United States" (p. 10). Goodwife Anita and Doctor Kroner, the supreme

26

manager who will decide the promotion and who, as a friend of his late father favors Paul, both feel that Proteus has not shown enough "drive" in pursuit of Pittsburgh. Dr. Lawson Shepherd, a passed-over classmate whom Paul calls "Dog-Eat-Dog," does his best to sabotage the promotion by dropping hints that Proteus' nerves are going, and with them his competency. It is the question of the promotion which gives impetus to Paul's soul-searching.

The company dinner-party at which Paul should seal his promotion brings an old friend, Ed Finnerty, to town. Ed has always been eccentric—unkempt and unconventional. He disrupts the dinner-party, announces he has resigned his high post in Washington, denounces and disgusts Anita, and takes Paul on a drinking binge in Homestead. There they meet anthropologist-cum-barfly-cum-RRC chaplain James Lasher, who impresses them both with his criticisms of the society. Ed, who is now hunted for disloyalty to the system and for having taken a long-forgotten rusty revolver from Paul, goes into hiding with Lasher, eventually becoming a founder of the Ghost Shirt Society, an underground organization dedicated to the overthrow of the technological society and the restoration of dignity to ordinary men. The increasingly doubting Paul toys with the idea of escape to an antiquated farm, but then finds himself designated as leader of the Blue Team at a rah-rah retreat on an island in the St. Lawrence. During the retreat it is proposed that Paul become double agent as a precondition to his promotion. He will be branded "saboteur," the most damning appelation possible in this society, ostracized, join the Ghost Shirt Society, and thus lead the police to Lasher and Finnerty. Since no one must know Paul's desertion is a ploy, even his wife reviles him, and Paul suffers the added humiliation of discovering that Anita has been having an affair with Dog-Eat-Dog Shepherd. Rather ironically, Paul has been hesitant right up to this point, and it seems likely that if he had not been forced into his double-agent role he might never have actually taken the step of joining the Ghost Shirt Society. Once driven out of the retreat, however, the break is made for him and he has no intention of performing the spy role.

Back in Ilium, Paul is scooped up by the Ghost Shirts and, as a former goldenboy of the system, is chosen as their messiah figure. The first meeting he attends, which reveals that his secretary Katherine Finch and the Ilium Works' boy-genius Bud Calhoun are Ghost Shirters, is raided, and Paul captured. When he refuses to play his assigned role as agent he is tried for treason. While the trial is in progress, however, the Ghost Shirt uprising takes place, the court is invaded and Paul liberated. The Ghost Shirt uprising proves fairly successful in Ilium and a few other cities, but is generally short-lived. Government forces surround Ilium, and robot helicopters announce that unless the leaders are surrendered in six hours the city will be besieged for six months, leaving the inhabitants to suffer in the midst of the desolation they have themselves created. Disillusioned by the facts that his Ghost Shirters have destroyed everything indiscriminately, that they are now enjoying themselves repairing the most senseless machines, and that his fellow leaders had been motivated egocentrically with no real expectation of success, Paul surrenders.

Around this central plot-line are woven the stories of secondary characters. The most important of these concerns the Shah of Bratpuhr, "spiritual leader of 6,000,000 members of the Kalhouri sect," who is on a state visit to the United States. Coming from a "more primitive" country, the Shah provides another and ironic perspective on this future society as he visits the "average home" of Edgar R. B. Hagstrohm, baffles the new wonder computer EPICAC XIV with a riddle, chats with Private Elmo Hacketts while inspecting the guard of honor, and picks up a distressed brunette on the streets of Homestead. In the end the Shah, taken for a shriner, is consigned to a foxhole during the Ghost Shirt uprising. Private Hacketts and Edgar R. B. Hagstrohm contribute to subplots of their own, and the Shah's guide, Dr. Ewing Halyard of the State Department, provides a subplot to the Shah's subplot. Halyard's troubles are not confined to explaining to the Shah the difference between citizens and slaves—a hard distinction in this era—or the inevitable provision of women for visiting dignitaries. For he has gained his Ph.D. on a computer error in a time when computers inevitably catch their own mistakes sooner or later. Halyard has not completed a college P.E. requirement. When this error is discovered, he is told to return to Cornell and make good the credits. But Dr. Roseberry, Cornell's athletic director (through whom we are taken into a digression on college athletics), has in his possession a letter Halyard once wrote to the college president criticizing Cornell's athletic policies. Needless to say, Halyard is subjected to a "make-up examination" which reduces him to a physical wreck—and which he flunks.

As the foregoing summary might suggest, there is no straightforward development of one plot in *Player Piano*. The story of Proteus' metamorphosis from company man to rebel should be central, but at times we are not sure that it remains so. The subplots and digressions often weaken the central narrative; Paul is not a fully convinced company man at the outset, and there are limitations to his rebellion at the end; and, above all, Vonnegut is obviously more interested in the actions of the whole society than of one man. One wonders if the Proteus-plot amounts to more than a vehicle for the story of a society which has reached the point of nightmare, attempts a faltering rebellion, and fails. There is some weakness, then, in the depth and even the consistency of the protagonist's characterization, and in the strength and unity of the plot. These things weaken *Player Piano* as a *novel*. On the other hand, they are things which probably contribute to the book's success in what it does best—present a broadly satirical view enlivened by comic episode, fanciful invention and suspense.

The central conflict in the novel is between the machine and the human, between those forces which have brought about and espouse automation and those which affirm the dignity of man, the warmth and fallibility of his animal being. Two central symbols appearing early in the story

29

focus this conflict. The first is a cat which Proteus is pleased to discover because a recent plant failure has been caused by mice gnawing an electric cable. When he goes to check the failure in Plant 58, he takes the cat with him. The cat becomes terrified of the robot cleaning machine and flees, but the mechanical hunter ruthlessly tracks her down and swallows up the animal predator. The animal, however, holds on to life tenaciously, miraculously emerges alive, and sprints for the fence. But even a cat only gets two lives in this mechanized world and the electrified wires atop the fence prove too much. "She dropped to the asphalt—dead and smoking, but outside" (p. 21). A triumph in defeat, of course, that anticipates the triumphant defeat of Proteus and the other revolutionaries who also give up their lives to break out of the system. The cat, then, becomes a symbol of animal life in a world of machines, foreshadowing the eventual ill-fated rebellion against total mechanization.

The other important symbol gives the book its title: the player piano. This instrument makes an appropriate symbol since it represents one of the oldest and seemingly most harmless attempts to duplicate and replace the movements of man by means of holes punched in paper. Proteus, Finnerty and Shepherd have followed this same procedure at the old Plant 58. They had measured the motions of Rudy Hertz, the best machine operator, and recorded them on tape. The machines now run themselves—albeit not quite as well as the newer ones—and Rudy becomes the replaced "piano player." When Paul stumbles upon the now old and somewhat senile Rudy in the Homestead tavern, the displaced operator insists on playing the player piano in honor of the engineer. Rudy regards the instrument with awe, saying, "You can almost see a ghost sitting there playing his heart out" (p. 38). The ghost that we see, and which Paul sees, of course, is of Rudy himself. Vonnegut underlines the already heavy irony by immediately beginning the next chapter with: " 'Darling, you look as though you've seen a ghost,' said Anita" (p. 38). So the player piano becomes the symbol of the machines that turn men into idle ghosts.

The player piano goes further than that as a symbol, however, for it also captures the ambiguity of the human attitude toward machines. Rudy's delight in the player piano recalls the scene, only a few pages earlier, in which Paul stands entranced by the "wild and Latin music" of the machines in Plant 58. Vonnegut's prose is seldom more lyrical than when describing Paul's reaction to that symphony of machine sounds. The music of machines emblematizes their appeal to the modern American male. Bud Calhoun, the master inventor, finds machines so fascinating that he inevitably invents one to replace himself. He also invents a device to tell the plant gate guards what to do in the case of each visitor: " 'Or we could tack a memo about policy on the guard house wall,' said Paul. Bud looked startled, 'Yes,' he said slowly, 'you *could* do thet' " (p. 80). Other examples of such love of machines abound. When Paul beats the robot "Checker Charley" and the machine, having been tampered with by Finnerty, collapses in flashing lights and smoke, the company men gathered to watch are full of sympathy for the robot. Even the barber who has nightmares of being replaced by a machine ends up dreaming the invention himself (p. 199). When Paul's car breaks down, there are "Reeks and Wrecks" anxious to tinker with the motor. And ultimately we see Bud Calhoun and a crowd of the rebels engrossed in fixing the very machines they have just smashed.

Vonnegut shows an understanding of this appeal of the machine, as well as obviously recognizing its danger. He seems intrigued by American ingenuity, the ability to invent, contrive, and keep things running, and rather nostalgically places its origins with the Yankee tinker. He makes fun of that fascination, frequently presenting it as a schoolboy delight in clockwork toys, but he also captures the appeal of machinery, which is why his satire appears richest when it deals with men and machines. The passage where the RRC man cuts a gasket for Paul's car out of his hat band, for example, makes fun of this displaced man's finding the motor so irresistible that he helps his enemy, of his self-assured act as he does it, and of the irony of the Works' manager being unable to fix a car, but it also projects the rather sentimental affection and respect for the improvising mechanic that Steinbeck accords his Okies urging their jalopies to California. A similar mixed feeling attends Paul's listening to the music of the machines. The descriptions of the music are comic —Vonnegut is pulling our legs and Paul's, too—yet the energy-charged music *is* "exciting," as if the author sees in it the kind of appeal to be found in scrap-iron sculpture. Such scenes work well because of their ambiguity—they mock and sympathize simultaneously. Machines are dangerous, Vonnegut suggests, in the hands of managers obsessed with efficiency, but it is the boyish, romantic love of gadgetry which gives birth to them. And the tinkers are not guiltless (as the frantic repairing at the end of the book emphasizes) if the managers make monsters of their toys.

Ed Finnerty, the brightest of the bright young men, emerges as the engineer most disaffected with machines. His engineering genius has taken him to a very high post in Washington, D.C., and has earned him classification E-022 (for scale, the Pope, if American, would be an R-001 while a bishop rates R-002), but he has rejected the spell of gadgetry. He it is who tampers with Checker Charley and who delights in hammering on the keys of the player piano. As if his name were not enough, he drinks Irish whiskey, making him a stereotyped unkempt, emotional Gaelic opposite of clean, scientific, Teutonic efficiency. (The top manager and engineer, significantly, have German names—Kroner and Baer.) Finnerty's characterization follows rather stereotyped lines in other ways, too. His nonconformity and Abe Lincoln looks stamp him the rugged individualist. His drinking, whoring, dirtiness and general rejection of the company man's suburban life style, and his spending his money on books, records and good whiskey rather than on cars and clothes, make him a set-piece anti-system intellectual. While his role as the "good-guy" hippie-engineer does undergo some complication as the novel progresses, initially it appears to be just what the plot demands by way of jogging Paul's conscience and focusing his discontent. Finnerty becomes the first powerful external force pulling Paul away from his dedication to the values of the automated era.

Our young Doctor Proteus has been wavering in his dedication before Finnerty arrives. In fact, Paul finds himself looking forward to Ed's visit as a source of moral support, but then he rather quickly becomes disenchanted with his old friend. For one thing, Paul has been thinking of Ed as a man who manages to preserve his independence while remaining a successful company man. He quickly learns, however, that Finnerty has quit his job and has become a complete outsider. That is more than Paul is prepared for at this point. Furthermore, Ed's insults to Anita, his grubbiness, his antisocial behavior at the dinner for the venerable Kroner, and his sabotaging of Checker Charley become distasteful to Paul and tend to drive him back from rebellion. He does not want to be like *that*. On the other hand, the company people irk Paul increasingly, and he does not want to be like them, either. The varying pressures they exert to keep Paul in line, to keep him competitive, ambitious, happy in the privilege of his class and content with his social world, tend to fuel his discontent.

Bud Calhoun, for example, courts Paul's secretary, Katherine Finch, mainly by sprawling on the couch in her office and drawling at her in a Southern accent. That he should eventually be replaced by his own machine seems appropriate—he has become a computer, mentally alive but physically inert, himself. (A motif throughout Vonnegut is that the more technological a society, the more machinelike its people become.) Bud's constant lounging presence and his boyish delight in machines—such as his gadget-laden car, a sort of diletante's Batmobile—annoy Paul. Although possessing the potential to invent a mechanical replacement for Paul himself, as he has for others, Calhoun poses no personal threat. It is Dr. Lawson ("Dog-Eat-Dog") Shepherd who looks most threatening. He feels passed over, and devotes himself to undermining his boss by spreading rumors of his failing nerves, criticizing his decisions, and occupying Paul's desk when he can to sign papers "in the absence of Dr. Proteus." The organization wants Paul to "give a damn," to want to advance. Shepherd does. And in Shepherd, Paul sees the worst of what technological business can make a man become. Rather than being goaded into competing and outpacing Shepherd as he easily could, he recoils and takes comfort in the secret assurance that he does *not* give a damn.

At home Paul faces the constant pushing of his ambitious wife, Anita, who is dedicated to being the perfect "woman behind the man." She collects information from the gossip mill of company wives, as well as from what Shepherd plants in her ear, gives Paul pep talks, writes out fact sheets for him and tries to pre-plan his interviews with his superiors. Example:

" . . . item III., A., I., a.: 'Don't smoke. Kroner is trying to break the habit.' " (p. 113)
Or:
" 'IV., A., I. If Kroner asks you why you want Pittsburgh, say it is because you can be of greater service , . . . a. Soft-pedal bigger house and raise and prestige.' " (p. 114)

Repeatedly throughout the story the husband and wife exchanges end with the ritual chorus and response: "I love you, Paul," "I love *you*, Anita." The formula seems empty—Anita is saying something she feels a good wife should say, just as she is studiedly glamorous, sexually inventive and socially polished because she feels a good wife should be. Paul satisfies convention while meaning "get off the phone and let me get back to work." Yet Paul *does* care for Anita. As readers we may cheer Finnerty's suggestion that she could easily be replaced by a stainless-steel and foam-rubber robot, and we recognize that through her Vonnegut mocks our stereotype of the upper-middle-class suburban wife. But for Paul she remains the one object of love, the only point of human warmth in a sterile world, and even at the end when she has betrayed him sexually, emotionally, and intellectually he still deeply regrets her loss.

At the start, then, Paul is a divided, uncertain man. On the one hand he loves his wife, though often for the

34

"wrong" reasons, mistaking her glossy magazine ideas for artistic temperament and her conventional social-climbing for intuitive wisdom. His fascination with machines is undeniable, and he has a conventional faith in the goodness of technological progress. His social orthodoxy makes him rankled by Calhoun's failure to rise when he enters the room and feel shocked by Finnerty's lack of hygiene. He is also in the process of writing an apparently standard speech on the Second Industrial Revolution, setting out all the usual platitudes about gains in efficiency and what a Utopia it realized for all. On the other hand, he feels vague misgivings. He has no intense desire for the promotion to manager of the Pittsburgh Works. His relationship with Anita has become clouded by uncertainty. "If her approach was disturbingly rational, systematic, she was thorough enough to turn out a creditable counterfeit of warmth. Paul could only suspect her feelings were shallow—and perhaps that suspicion was part of what he was beginning to think of as his sickness" (p. 25). His uncertainty is of that kind—not sharply identifiable doubts about his world, but vague, haunting suspicions which he cannot be sure are more than his own neurosis. Discussing his speech with his secretary, he can defend the industrial progress intellectually, but reflect that under the old system there was "happiness, too" (p. 22). He tries to tell himself that life really has been improved, and ponders that if he had served in the war he might now have more conviction.

> Maybe he'd be able to understand then how good everything now was by comparison, to see what seemed so clear to others—that what he was doing, had done, and would do as manager and engineer was vital, above reproach, and had, in fact, brought a golden age. Of late, his job, the system, and organized politics had left him variously annoyed, bored, or queasy. (pp. 14-15)

The mixture of feeling is well drawn. It is important to the novel to have Paul divided in this way. Rejection of the system by a man never committed to it, such as Finnerty, carries less weight. Paul's wavering adds tension to a story which otherwise might become a too easily one-sided attack, contributes most of what dimension there is to his characterization, and affords the author the opportunity to explain his position through the arguments and events which finally persuade Paul.

Those arguments and events which turn Proteus from the fair-haired boy of the system to the messiah of the rebellion naturally form the basis of the social criticism in the novel. That criticism becomes far-ranging, frequently taking in all too familiar targets—a father indifferent to his children, rah-rah overgrown-fraternity-boy-businessmen, the "Mrs. Robinson" style upper-middle-class wife, the army, etc. In fact, the satire in *Player Piano* sometimes seems strangely dated, even for 1952. Perhaps then America looked forward technologically but backward emotionally. Certainly the argument has often been advanced that one reason for the election of President Eisenhower in that year is that people longed for the peace, tranquility and stability which they felt he represented. But, even for 1952, much in the novel seems rather old-fashioned and to look backward. The "Gee, swell," language of the businessmen and engineers, for example, sounds a lot like Sinclair Lewis' *Babbitt* of 1922. The retreat on the St. Lawrence rather resembles the convention Babbitt attends, and one finds an occasional touch of Steinbeck in the description of the "Reeks and Wrecks." Yet these echoes of the past are appropriate in *Player Piano,* first, because the novel does in part ask, "where did we go wrong?" and measure present and future gains against things of the past lost, and second, because nostalgia is the source of much of Paul's earlier reflection.

From its opening, this novel of the future emphasizes the past. Ilium straddles the Iroquois River, and by the third page its past history of battles between Mohawks and Algonquins, Dutch and Mohawks, British and Dutch, Americans and British, and the continued existence of pioneer names like van Zandt and Courtland, have been noted. Paul's interest in the past emerges quickly and we learn that he "sometimes wondered if he wouldn't have been more content in another period of history . . ."

(p. 12). He has preserved Building 58 as a sort of working museum, since it was established by Edison in 1886: "It was a vote of confidence from the past, he thought—where the past admitted how humble and shoddy it had been, where one could look from the old to the new and see that mankind had come a long way. Paul needed that reassurance from time to time" (p. 14). In the building, Paul feels soothed by the carved initials on the walls and the adze-hewn rafters. Looking at photographs of old works' teams, he notes the pride in the eyes of the workers, be they sweepers or inspectors—those now replaced by machines or those now become the managerial elite—and feels a vague sense of loss. And he remembers how, as a fresh young engineer, he had helped record the motions of Rudy Hertz, the best machinist, and thus set up the automated plant. Building 58, the one part of the factory Paul seems genuinely to care about and to which he retreats for solace, provides him with a link to an earlier period of history for which he feels nostalgia, and also affords him a connection with his own youth, full of enthusiasm, innocence and faith. Whether this backward looking is the cause of Paul's hesitancy, or whether his doubts about his present situation lead to the nostalgia, remains somewhat elusive, but the former probably predominates. We see Paul several times measure the present against the past and his sense of loss, of uncertainty about the direction of the present, grows each time he does so. As the tension within him increases, his identification with the old machines in Building 58 becomes obvious. " 'Basically, it wasn't built for the job it's doing anway. . . . ' " he tells Katherine.

> "I look for the buzzer to go off any day now, and that'll be the end."
> In each meter box, in addition to the instrument, the jewel, and the warning lamp, was a buzzer. The buzzer was the signal for a unit's complete breakdown. (p. 25)

So Paul's "complete breakdown," when it comes, derives to a considerable degree from a nostalgia, from a sense of once-good things being annihilated by the spread of automation. Much of the "anti-progress" sentiment expressed by characters in the novel and by the book itself is of the same sort. The latter point should be qualified at once, lest its obviousness be misunderstood. The criticism of this mechanized Utopia *could* be primarily from the point of view of measuring it against the kind of Utopia men should aspire to or that Vonnegut might advocate. Instead, the past provides the standard. This distinction becomes important when one considers that this future world of the novel is used to characterize and interpret the present. It suggests that, inasmuch as we share Vonnegut's misgivings about the directions of the present, we do so less from a sense that things are not progressing toward our ideal adequately than from a feeling that the good things of a mixed past are being lost. Paul recognizes the significance of remembrance of former times to the measuring of the present when he tells Katherine, " 'It's fresh to you because you're too young to know anything but the way things are now' " (p. 22). His rebellion, in consequence, can be seen as essentially conservative in nature. This aspect of his impulse emerges strongly when he feels tempted to resolve his doubts by retreating to the old Gottwald farm. The Gottwald (God's-Wood?) place obviously contrasts with the story's other retreat, the company boost-session at the Meadows. Haycox, the caretaker of the farm, is an old-world type who effectively pours scorn on the newfangled world of machines and Ph.D.s: " 'I'm a doctor of cowshit, pigshit, and chickenshit,' he said. 'When you doctors figure out what you want, you'll find me out in the barn shoveling *my* thesis' " (p. 151). Paul loves "this completely authentic microcosm of the past . . ." and old Haycox who "might have been part of a pageant recalling farm life as it had once been" (p. 149). Nowhere does his nostalgia show more tellingly than in this episode.

Reliance on the past for solace and as standard flourishes among those left behind by progress. The Miami barber's long sermon to the Shah of Bratpuhr harps on the way things once were:

"Used to be there was a lot of damn fool things a dumb bastard could do to be great, but the machines fixed that. You know, used to be you could go to sea on a big clipper ship or a fishing ship and be a big hero in a storm." (p. 198)

A fully automated and hygienic bar in Homestead proves truly a nine-day wonder, but the "dust and germ trap of a Victorian bar" provides just the right echo of the past. Rudy Hertz lives on the memory of having had the best hands of any machinist, and drinks "to old times." Others in the Homestead bar divide by age and memory: "The youngsters in the booth, the two soldiers and three girls, they were like Katherine Finch. They couldn't remember when things had been different, could hardly make sense of what had been, though they didn't necessarily like what was. But these others who stared now, they remembered." (p. 35). The situation has its comic aspects, of course, and some things have not changed. Sitting in the bar, Paul, Finnerty, and Lasher discuss the rigidity of the social hierarchy, determined by IQ tests and academic achievement graphs, but conclude it can still be penetrated by sex appeal and nepotism. " 'Big tits will get you in anywhere,' said Finnerty. 'Well, it's comforting to know that something hasn't changed in centuries, isn't it?' Lasher smiled" (p. 95). Lasher leans on the past, of course, not just for comfort but also to give the rebellion he inspires respectability. As a minister he draws heavily on traditional religious symbology, and as a social scientist he draws on past cultural patterns. He it is who conceives of "The Ghost Shirt Society," named after a nineteenth century Indian uprising. (The Society's title effectively connects with the "ghosts" of displaced men mentioned earlier [p. 38].) The Indian ghost-shirters had also been men rendered useless and hopeless by a changed society who made one last desperate and futile effort to defend "the old values." Even the revolutionaries, then, draw their myths from the past and fight for an old world rather than a new. They are, in fact, counter-revolutionaries, dedicated to undoing much brought by the Second Industrial Revo-

39

lution and to barring the course of the Third, now in progress.

On the other side of the fence, such leaders of technological "progress" as Kroner and Baer are also sentimental about the past. These two favor Paul largely because of his father, and revere Checker Charley not just out of the general reverence for machines but from respect for Berringer's father, "one of the top computing-machine men in the country," who had built it. Sentimentalism over the past, personal and social, pervades their approach to the retreat at the Meadows. Kroner and Baer recapture their younger days—indeed, seem to indulge a second childhood—as they compete in sports, shout slogans, and sing team songs. Sentimental old lyrics— "My Wild Irish Rose" and "Love's Sweet Song"—set much of the mood of the retreat, and there is an absolute outpouring of formularized emotion when the company men gather around the sacred Oak, symbol of their organization, to remember the dear departed. The sense that "this is our custom, this is the traditional way we do things here," permeates the retreat. Regeneration, which is at least the intended function of this circus, is drawn out of the past. Just as Paul had sought to feel the past's approval of current progress in the old Edison-established building (p. 56), so the company managers use the past to give respectability to their actions. One of the theatrics at the Meadows involves a fake Indian chief giving his blessing to the young technicians: " 'Now our braves are gone . . . But the spirit of my people lives on, the Spirit of the Meadows' " (p. 213). (Both rebels and company men, then, use the Indian past to give dignity to their causes.) Another theatrical consists of a trite melodrama in which Young Engineer wins average man John from the persuasions of the Radical by pointing out how much better he lives now than he did when he worked. Part of the Young Engineer's argument insists that John has more than Caesar, Napoleon or Henry VIII could dream of. The way of the machines is the good old American way.

Evaluation of this futuristic society from the perspective of the past enters into the novel in another important way through the Shah of Bratpuhr. Fantasy or science fiction frequently makes use of an outside observer from another society, planet, or time period who, from his fresh perspective, exposes the foibles of the depicted society. In science fiction, in particular, the outsider often comes from a more advanced planet and finds the pretensions of humans ludicrous, their most complex technology, crude. The Shah, as the alien observer in *Player Piano*, represents the opposite extreme. He visits America from a technologically less developed state, and his perspective is one of naïveté coupled with a kind of primitive wisdom. Since he comes from an old and scarcely changing society of "slaves and elite," he can, in effect, voice the judgment of the past on the wonders of this mechanized America. The Shah perceives the basic, perennial social pattern at the heart of new systems, and tests the pretensions of the innovators with his earthy view of essential human needs and desires. Hence his insistence on calling the "citizens" of the electronic Utopia "slaves," and on translating this non-competitive ultimate in centrally managed capitalism as "communism." The Shah tours the country puncturing its balloons since what he is shown are the things in which this new America takes most pride but which are consequently the most vulnerable to his down-to-earth valuations. Reconstruction and Reclamation Corpsmen, soldiers, the writer's wife he picks up, the family whose home he is shown through, all are *"Takaru"*—slaves. His State Department guide carefully explains that they are *not* slaves, but citizens. At first the Shah thinks the terms are interchangeable, for a while is puzzled by Halyard's insistence that they are not, but ends comfortably convinced that all the "ci-ti-zens" he sees are, indeed, *"Takaru."* His judgment maddens his guides, but we see the rightness of it. The RRCmen, condemned by their IQs to spending their lives watching each other perform make-work jobs, have no more freedom than slaves. When one spits in Halyard's face, the Shah observes sympathetically that " 'it is the same with *Takaru* everywhere since the war' " (p. 29). Another *Takaru* is Private Hacketts, who takes pride in being in the army, not the "Reeks and

41

Wrecks," but who also knows that his IQ prevents his promotion, and lives for the day twenty three years hence when, as a civilian, he can tell a general to "Kiss my —." The Shah sees another unchanging pattern here, and comments that " 'Americans have changed almost everything on earth, . . . but it would be easier to move the Himalayas than to change the Army' " (p. 71). In his visit to the home of the *Takaru,* the Shah sees Edgar and Wanda Hagstrohm so surrounded by time-saving devices and security that their lives have no interest or purpose. When the Shah asks what Wanda is supposed to do in all the saved time, he is told she can " 'Live! Get a little fun out of life!' " And what does she do? " 'Oh television,' she mumbled. 'Watch that a lot, don't we, Ed? And I spend a lot of time with the kids. . .' " (p. 160) But it emerges that Wanda has been washing clothes in the tub for a month, because the washer has broken down, and enjoying it for the sake of something to do. The Shah does not miss the point and, patting the machines, he chuckles, *"Brahuana!"*—or "live."

In these episodes, the Shah exposes familiar and easy targets, especially in the Army and the Hagstrohm family. His perspective is one which the reader shares, and we enjoy his debunking of what his hosts present as the good life. He exposes what we all hold suspect in the human consequences of automation, in the military mentality, in the proliferation of labor-saving gadgetry, and in the middle-class home life. The guide showing the Shah the wonders of the mechanized home comes off a little like Richard Nixon protesting the merits of American kitchens to Chairman Khrushchev. The Hagstrohms, after all, represent an all too familiar pattern: the husband bored and unchallenged, having an affair which only increases his anxiety; the wife bored with a home routine of dishes, kids and TV. The Shah provides a vehicle for comic deflation of the prosperous American life, and from his outsider's viewpoint, tells us what we already know: that all's not for the best in the best of all possible worlds. The comedy of his observations comes largely from the fact that he appears not to comprehend anything. Certainly

42

he does not understand things in the terms he is meant to, the terms of "the establishment." As Halyard says, " 'This guy thinks of everything he sees in terms of his own country, and his own country must be a Goddamn mess' " (p. 71). But, of course, the Shah does comprehend on a more important basic level, and hence the comedy and wisdom of his commentary which at once misinterprets and pins down the essence of things.

There are two other episodes involving the Shah which deserve attention, both for their interest in this particular context and as forerunners of themes Vonnegut returns to subsequently. The first involves the writer's wife whom the Shah picks up in Harrisburg. She offers herself since her husband, having "failed" as a novelist and refused public relations duty, has no income. The acceptance of his first novel would have raised him from a W-441 (fiction novice) to a W-440 (fiction journeyman) or a W-225 (public relations). But the novel was refused by the National Council of Arts and Letters for being twenty-seven pages too long, too intellectual, and having an anti-machine theme.

> "This husband of yours, he'd rather have his wife a—
> Rather, have her—" Halyard cleared his throat—"than go into
> public relations?"
> "I'm proud to say," said the girl, "that he's one of the few
> men on earth with a little self-respect left." (p. 234)

To which the Shah can only comment, sadly, that "some of the greatest prophets were crazy as bed bugs." It is an episode in which Vonnegut can undercut both sides of the issue: the attitudes of the society toward art and the writer's ivory-towerism. Halyard's explanations of the twelve book clubs to meet twelve types of readers, "readability quotients" (to prevent books from being too literary) and market surveys, of the Dog Story of the Month and novels of "the old days on the Erie Canal" mass printed at less cost than seven packs of chewing gum, expose a barren culture where fiction is marketed like aspirin. We recognize that culture as a hyperbolic rendition of our own and see, as we shall again and again in the fiction that follows, Vonnegut commenting on the plight of the novelist (or of himself, in effect) in his choices between artistic integrity and publishing success. Ed, the brunette's husband, stands by integrity. He will not go into public relations, he will not write about the approved subjects because "he never got mad at clipper ships or the Erie Canal," and he will not be tranquilized by psychiatry because he believes somebody must be "maladjusted" and ask questions. All of which Vonnegut seems to applaud. But Ed's integrity ends where his wife's prostitution begins, or at least becomes questionable, as the Shah's remark about prophets being crazy as bed bugs (another recurrent theme in Vonnegut) points out. There are foreshadowings here of those passages where Vonnegut speaks of his own short stories as commercial undertakings to support his novel writing or discusses the merits of novelists and science fiction writers. He seems compelled to muse on the conflicting demands the writer feels, often in a way which invites speculation as to what he might imply about his own role. We shall return to this topic later.

The second episode involving the Shah which points to things to come occurs when he visits the Carlsbad Caverns, brain center of the body mechanical. Here are assembled the EPICAC computers, including the stupendous new EPICAC XIV, which survey markets, set production, test military contingency plans, supervise placement of personnel and generally run the country. President Lynn tells the Shah that EPICAC XIV is "the greatest individual in history, that the wisest man that had ever lived was to EPICAC XIV as a worm was to the wisest man" (p. 119). This proves too much of a challenge for the Shah, who tells how his people expect someday the arrival of an all-wise god whose identity will be known by his ability to solve the riddle which he now puts to EPICAC:

"Silver bells shall light my way,
And nine times nine maidens fill my day,
And mountain lakes will sink from sight,
And tigers' teeth will fill the night." (p. 121)

But as the President says, "You can't just talk to it." And the Shah's riddle cannot be punched out and coded, so mighty EPICAC fails to identify itself as the one whose coming will end all suffering on earth. *"Baku!"* says the Shah—"false god." Besides underlining the spiritual and imaginative paucity of the technology-worshipping society, the episode introduces us to the family of EPICACs who inhabit Vonnegut's stories, to machines who plan and play, write poetry, fall in love, commit suicide, and even become the closest thing to an Omnipotent Power that we see in Vonnegut's world.

While the Shah of Bratpuhr sees from the start the spiritual poverty, the emotional deadness, and the social hypocrisy of this future America, Paul Proteus comes only falteringly to the same recognition. To his own vague dissatisfactions and uncertainties have been added arguments of Finnerty and Lasher, his new awareness of the lives of the average citizen through his visits to Homestead, his glimpse of another way of life at the old Gottwald farm, and his increasing revulsion from the style of the management class, intensified at the retreat. But it takes some heavy last straws to break the back of his resistance to joining the Ghost Shirters. Being asked to turn informer on his friend, Ed Finnerty" (p. 132). Even Chirt Society proves the turning point: "For once, his dissatisfaction with his life was specific. He was reacting to an outrage that would be regarded as such by almost any man in any period in history. He had been told to turn informer on his friend, Ed Finnerty" (p. 132). Even then his intent and his resolve remain undercut. He makes sure first that he is "in excellent shape to afford integrity. . . ," having a personal fortune of three quarters of a million dollars. Secondly, he hesitates in a way which seems endearingly human if somewhat obtuse when it comes to Anita, believing "She was what fate had given him to love, and he did his best to love her" (p. 133). He again resolves to reeducate this obviously unchangeable woman, and *then* resign to a private life. Events, however, force his hand. When he gives his superiors his resignation they think that he is simply playing his assigned

45

espionage role with enthusiasm, so that again his options remain open. But as he leaves the island retreat he blunders upon Anita in the arms of Dog-Eat-Dog Shepherd. Their marriage essentially comes to an end with a new increment of the old refrain:

"I like you. Don't forget that ever."
"And I like *you*, Anita." (p. 238)

Then, after a week's isolation at home, Paul goes to the Homestead bar where he is drugged and secreted into the Ghost Shirt Society. He has hesitated "for want of a blow severe enough to knock him off the course dictated by the circumstances of his birth and training" (p. 178-9), and it takes a succession of fairly severe blows to make him take his stand.

Proteus' hesitation might seem hard to understand considering all he has seen and heard, but in fact is probably one of the most plausible aspects of the novel given his past values and upbringing, and the consequences—loss of position, wife and home, criminal prosecution possibly ending in a death sentence for sabotage—of his action. Expecting Paul to forsake all he has grown up doing and believing and to oppose it is almost like asking a bank president to become an anarchist bomber. He learns gradually. His attempts to explain to Anita are faltering:

"In order to get what we've got, Anita, we have, in effect, traded these people out of what was the most important thing on earth to them—the feeling of being needed and useful, the foundation of self-respect. . . . Darling, when I see what we've got, and then see what these people have got, I feel like a horse's ass" (p. 169).

When, later, Anita objects and asks what else people could want to be given, he tries to explain that *being given* everything is just what is wrong:

"Hell, everybody used to have some personal skill or willingness to work or something he could trade for what he wanted.

46

Now that the machines have taken over, it's quite somebody who has anything to offer. All most people can do is hope to be given something" (p. 177).

The core of Paul's beliefs, and the basis of his defense at his trial, is contained in the long letter written by Professor von Neumann but published over Paul's signature. The letter advocates that machines and organization be relegated to their proper function of assisting man, that the wishes and well-being of men be considered before efficiency, and that imperfection be recognized as a virtue, since man is imperfect and man is a creation of God. Paul stands by this creed, and when imprisoned and asked by Kroner to name the leader of the Ghost Shirt Society, he replies that he is—taking his stand at last. "The instant he'd said it, he knew it was true, and knew what his father had known—what it was to belong and believe" (p. 293).

The human virtue of imperfection, of course, proves to be the undoing of the Ghost Shirt uprising, of which Paul is the messiah. Various uprisings across the country prove premature and poorly organized. As von Neumann concludes, "the theory of attack was essentially valid. The execution, of course, was something else again" (p. 309). A key failure is that of the Salt Lake saboteurs to knock out EPICAC. Their scheme proves too tricky—they try to blow up the Caverns by putting nitroglycerine in the coke bottles of a vending machine. Such failures of the revolution resemble those of the technological order they hope to bring down in their obsession with gadgetry and complexity. Bud, for instance, again shows his love for technology by inventing some immensely complex machine to penetrate the Ilium Works, and is deflated when someone suggests simply cutting through the fence. But the virtue of imperfection best characterizes the revolt, contributing to its failure while at the same time remaining its chief affirmation. For in their mistakes and blunders, the Ilium men affirm, more than they realize, the principle that humans are imperfect and that imperfection is human. To win, to prove more efficient and organized than the

47

machine society would, in one sense, amount to a greater defeat. Thus we see the revolutionaries getting drunk, indiscriminately destroying all machines and plants, including those vital to their own life-support, disregarding orders and planning, and finally amusing themselves repairing machines—reasserting the mentality they set out to destroy.

While the collapse of the uprising demonstrates the human virtue of imperfection, it does not emerge as an unqualified example of the classic "triumph in defeat." Human they may be, but the imperfections remain as genuine flaws. The ignorance, disorganization and short-sightedness of the machine wreckers are forgivable in context, but nevertheless remain exasperating. They are the reasons why the uprising seems doomed even before it begins, and for the tone of weary resignation of the last days. Even the intellectually more capable leaders seem flawed by the end. Bud, who has been replaced once by his own mechanical creation, remains unable to resist contriving gadgets. Von Neumann sees the revolution in abstract terms and is delighted with the experiment, apparently caring little for the people involved and the actual consequences to their lives. The same can be said of Lasher and Finnerty, the former satisfied with martyrdom and the creation of a symbolic gesture, the latter appeased by having struck at those who had personally rejected him. Only to Paul does the reality of the situation seem to mean anything, yet even his position is somewhat undercut. Nostalgia for the days of his youth remains his strongest motivation: " 'You know,' said Paul at last, 'things wouldn't have been so bad if they'd stayed the way they were when we first got here [Ilium]. Those were passable days, weren't they?' " (p. 312). And he and Finnerty indulge in reminiscence, recapturing the joys of inventing and mechanizing and automating, until they end up having gone full circle, with Paul saying:

"Most fascinating game there is, keeping things from staying the way they are."
"If only it weren't for people, the goddamned people," said

Finnerty, "always getting tangled up in machinery. If it weren't for them, earth would be an engineer's paradise." (p. 313)

Like the people of Ilium, whose eagerness "to recreate the same old nightmare" prevents Paul from making his toast "to a better world," the two engineers remain trapped in the dichotomy of embracing the process which creates the slavery they reject. Finally, Paul can only shrug and drink "to the record"—a record he scarcely comprehends and probably does not believe in.

Player Piano ends with no untarnished heroes and no unqualified affirmation in its resolution. It could hardly be called a hopeful book. The connections between present American society and the exaggeration of it Vonnegut projects in his future are so direct that it implies a vision of society in which there is little optimism. Yet neither is the novel entirely negative. Even its most unpleasant characters can be forgiven, or at least accepted with understanding. Shepherd has some justification in thinking he has been passed over, partly through nepotism, and his most contemptible behavior is really only a dogged pursuit of the values of the system he has been brought up to believe in. Anita also tries too hard, but we understand why when we realize that only marriage to Paul has saved her from Homestead. Kroner and Baer are boors who can be held responsible for considerable suffering, yet both are essentially good-hearted and well intentioned. And the smug Berringer, the immature engineer who tries to impress his superiors by using the robot to beat Paul at checkers and who has the habit of turning up smirking in Paul's worst moments, is too small, too pathetic, to earn much more than a mild contempt. On the other hand, the minor heroics of the more sympathetic characters do deserve some respect. Even Alfy, the TV shark, can be admired for his individuality and his pride in using his wits to follow an independent course. There is also Fred Garth—"willing, good-hearted, but apologetically weak, used up"—who finally makes his act of defiance by ring-barking the retreat's sacred oak. Finnerty, Lasher, and

Professor von Neumann all give their lives for a cause, the rightness of which we believe in, and they articulate that cause creditably, even if some questions remain about their personal motivations. Compared with these, however, Proteus earns our greater respect even though he never seems to equal their revolutionary conviction and fervor. Repeatedly he inclines toward evasion, and his nostalgia does not provide the most substantial base for a revolutionary stand. Yet he does make that stand. In fact, Paul probably has more to lose by so doing than any of the other leaders. And while Paul must undergo the most testing changes and most drastic reversals of values to become a revolutionary, and never becomes as articulate as the other leaders in espousing his cause, he ultimately shows the most genuine human compassion, purity of conscience, and pragmatic sense of purpose. Only at the last does he overcome his naïveté about the actions and motivations of his colleagues, but his final disillusioned vision is unclouded by the narrow idealism or the egocentric motivations of von Neumann, Lasher, and Finnerty.

At least one engineer-manager, then, has been awakened and has turned against an inhuman system. That is positive in spite of the noted qualifications of his resistance. The uprising fails and the Ghost Shirters fall short on a number of counts. Yet against this negative cast to the ending must be weighed the fact that the rebellion *does* occur at all and that men *do* rise to fight oppression and *do* sacrifice themselves for their beliefs. The final affirmative language of the novel must be assessed in this mixed context.

> Von Neumann considered Paul and then the broken glass. "This isn't the end, you know," he said. "Nothing ever is, nothing ever will be—not even Judgment Day."
> "Hands up," said Lasher almost gaily. "Forward March." (p. 320)

How are we to take the affirmative language here? Is it a throw-away ending? Is it ironic? Even cynical? Von Neumann's promise that this is not the end provides affirmation mainly in metaphor, and there may appear little substance to support it. And the notion that *nothing* is ever the end conjures up a wearying, meaningless continuum which devalues "the record" to which they drink. Yet the statement that this is not the end, with its implication that next time or sometime good men may win, *is* made. Lasher's "Forward March," with its significant capitals, ends the book with an old clarion call, a positive note. But it is rhetoric, and may be only that, and we know that its particular meaning for Lasher is that he welcomes death as martyrdom, as another symbolic gesture. Against both remarks, too, must be weighed Paul's inability, immediately before, to toast a better world. Paul's hope for a better world fades when he thinks of the people of Ilium, when he remembers the facts of what has happened: the cheer of his colleagues stems from viewing these events as metaphor or symbol. In the same terms, any optimism at the end of the book derives from figurative language: the facts provide little hope. Rather as with Sartre's *Les Jeux Sont Fait,* we are left feeling things will always turn out the same way, and that the author has been smiling wearily at another demonstration of man's inadequacy in the face of the universe.

In some ways, *Player Piano* proves the most difficult of Vonnegut's novels to assess. It seems the least settled, the least consistent to a form or mold. Initially it may strike us as another socio-moral analysis of the present through the future in the tradition of *The Time Machine, Brave New World* or *1984.* But then the resemblance shows shifts in the direction of the more immediate kinds of social criticism, like *Babbitt, Main Street* or even *The Grapes of Wrath.* Furthermore, comic episodes become frequent, sometimes roughly in the social-satiric vein of Aldous Huxley or Evelyn Waugh, sometimes as pure slapstick, sometimes almost of the comic strip guffaw-inducing variety. These references to other works and writers should not be taken to imply that Vonnegut is highly derivative, but simply to suggest the mixture present in this novel. *Player Piano* makes a great many points

51

about human behavior in general, about the unpredictable quirks of life itself, about society and its institutions. But perhaps Vonnegut is a little too intent on making all of these points. Be that the cause or not, the book remains somewhat unsettled and fragmented, never quite cohering into a consistent, sustained form.

The novel seems curiously mixed in other ways. Much of its social criticism is well aimed, and probably likely to win more friends while giving less offense in 1972 than it did in 1952, when faith in technology, science and the capitalistic system ran higher. The attacks on social ills obviously grow out of a deep compassion, and we sense the gentleness of this writer who so often portrays violence. On the other hand, the targets of the satire are frequently easy ones, some of them struck many times before, and the gentleness occasionally gives rise to rather awkward sentimentality. The "booster" businessman, the materialistic suburban wife, the adolescent lodge member, the too-eager junior executive, the army, the shamateur college athletic program, have all been thoroughly picked over before. The excessive sentimentality emerges where Vonnegut overloads a situation to emphasize its pathos. Episodes like those describing the unemployed watching a little boy float a paper boat down the gutter, or the RRC man proving his good old Yankee ingenuity, or Rudy Hertz's short-sighted pride in how he earned his redundancy, fall into this category.

Sentimentality, in right proportion or excess, emerges naturally in a novel which places so much emphasis on nostalgia. Here again one senses an ambivalence of feeling, but in this context Vonnegut uses both sentimentalism and ambivalence effectively. For while nostalgia is an understandable response to the fast-changing world, it should be indulged in only with caution. In fact, Vonnegut appears equally insistent in showing the limitations of both nostalgia and an avid faith in progress or futurity. The shortcomings of an unqualified belief in change for its own sake, constant technological development and a materially realized Utopia are made obvious throughout. The dangers implicit in nostalgia reveal themselves with more subtlety.

52

The attraction of the Gottwald farm for Paul demonstrates the regressive tendencies in such yearnings after the past. Paul's finding continuity in the old machines, photographs and carved initials of Plant 58 looks healthy enough, but his attitudes toward the farm are different. Haycox is right to regard Paul with some suspicion. The engineer sees the farm as a "microcosm of the past, a pageant recalling farm life as it had once been" (p. 149). His attitude, in the final analysis, seems little better than that of Anita, who regards the farm as a ready store of antiques. Proteus wants to escape the anxieties of his present life, to opt out of an uncertain situation into the safety of the past. It is a simplistic, impossible dream, because Anita could never adjust to such a life, because Paul himself could never thrive on shoveling manure, and because problems are never solved by such evasions. Paul eventually acts because he cannot betray a friend or deny his conscience. Personal escape, whether it be into a regressive psychological withdrawal or into some kind of physical isolation, leaves conscience and responsibility, as well as the problems, unanswered. In the later novels, Vonnegut develops this thesis repeatedly and explicitly as he shows one character after another retreat physically, mentally or temporally from the realities of the present. On balance, Vonnegut handles the topic well in *Player Piano*, the appeal of nostalgia giving the more dramatic emphasis to its dangers.

Stylistically, the novel again is mixed. It possesses the characteristic rapidity of Vonnegut's prose, induced in large part by the brevity of everything—sentences, paragraphs, chapters, even the book itself. The characterizations establish themselves quickly, often by fitting into familiar stereotypes. While there is an element of suspense to the central story, actions occur in rapid succession and with plenty of gusto. The episodic nature of the novel sometimes works against the rapid pace. We may chafe at plodding through a fairly stock satire of college athletics when we want to know if a new American revolution will succeed. The language of the book sometimes disappoints. It includes some journalistic, near-trite imagery, like the description of the young woman "with bosoms like balloon spinnakers before the wind" (the same simile was used to describe Ursula Andress in a popular magazine movie review), and some old-fashioned dialogue, too obviously contrived so as to stereotype the speakers:

"Hi, there, folks," he said. "Everything hunky-dory in my little old home, eh?"
Jimmy exchanged glances with his mother, and smiled oddly. "Yes sir, reckon it is. I mean, you're darn right it is!" (p. 248)

Some of this seems to be done intentionally as a spoofing on a familiar style in American fiction, but too often there are no signals to make us feel sure. At times the carry-over connections become too obvious, as in the "ghost" repetition linking chapters III and IV:

"You can almost see a ghost sitting there . . ."
"Darling, you look as though you've seen a ghost . . ." (p. 38)

By their very obviousness and unpretentiousness, such devices can assume an air of posed quaintness, becoming "camp" and comic, but the pattern for this is not as well established as in later novels, and not all of the bad spots can be made to go away.

The humor within the book proves one of its conspicuous strengths. One important comic device which Vonnegut pursues beyond *Player Piano* is the selection of names. Here we have Proteus, whose name implies quick changes of appearance or principle. Paul does change his dress every time he goes to Homestead, but the irony of the name arises because his change of principles is slow and painful. Finnerty's name brands him the free-wheeling Irishman—there may be a ludicrous echo of "finicky" in it, too. Moralist-satirist Lasher really does lash out at Ilium society. Anita is a "man-eater," besides being "neater." Ilium contrasts ironically with its namesake in Homer; and there are many other examples. Another passage employing an obvious technique to comic effect is the long alphabetical list of wrecked machinery in riot-

54

torn Ilium: ". . . air conditioners, amplidynes, analyzers, arc welders, batteries, belts, billers, . . ." and so it goes for almost a page (pp. 315-6). Comic episodes (Bud's inventing himself out of a job), comic exaggeration (the description of the retreat), comic preposterousness (Bud's car), comic double-meaning (" 'You'd need some kind of sensin' element that could smell a mouse.' 'Or a rat.' ") abound—but to explore them all might be too much like explaining a joke. *Player Piano*, for all its warnings and weariness and nostalgia, remains a funny book. But the mixture of pain and humor results in the kind of comedy which arises when people seek to make light of frightening situations, so that here, too, the novel sustains its peculiar tension.

Vonnegut suggests in *Player Piano* that our present society has much wrong with it and that unless things change it is likely to become even worse. Yet he also raises some questions about the likelihood of change. Bud Calhoun reverts to technology worship. Finnerty seems happy just to have shaken a society which he did not like and which did not like him. Von Neumann appears satisfied by "a fascinating experiment," and Lasher is content to have created a symbol. Even Proteus cannot drink "to a better world," as if convinced man's aspirations are of the sort that can only end in more nightmare. It is interesting to compare this ending, and the view it implies, with that of the roughly contemporary British novel, *Lord of the Flies*. William Golding concludes that book rather similarly, with a non-resolution which implies the beginning of another cycle of horrors—or at best, continuation. Marooned boys are saved from their private war on a boat-shaped island to be taken into the world of global war on a cruiser. Golding tends in *Lord of the Flies* to go behind the modern romantic's notion that the world is perfectable and knowable through science, and the older romantic view that man is good but society is corrupting. If society or the system corrupts, Golding argues, it is because evil lurks within man. In *Player Piano*, Kurt Vonnegut suggests that the system is corrupting, and that he is not very sure about man, either. Yet there is something

—perhaps the rather sentimental portrayals of Haycox, Rudy Hertz, or Fred Garth, for instance, or the use of well-intentioned but humanly imperfect men where there might have been villains—which suggests that Vonnegut blames the system more than the people, for all that he shows those people already rebuilding the most senseless of the machines they have just wrecked. Golding and Vonnegut are akin, however, in that both suggest that it is futile for man to keep looking outside of himself for the formula for a better world. Golding tells us that the beast is within; Vonnegut implies that to strive for a better world in perfecting the physical conditions of that world in "keeping things from staying the way they are," is to go from nightmare to nightmare. The answer to the meaning of life lies within each man, and it is futile to search on this planet, or to reach out to others, for the answer to "what all creation was all about." But for Vonnegut's development of this concept we must turn to *The Sirens of Titan.*

II

The Sirens of Titan:
Existential Science Fiction

In *Player Piano* that insufferable young engineer Berringer, dismayed by the destruction of Checker Charley, asks, "Why did it have to happen?" The author comments, "It was one more hollow echo to the question humanity had been asking for milleniums, the question men were seemingly born to ask" (p. 63). Finnerty's flippant answer to the existential "why" is Biblical: "The Lord giveth and the Lord taketh away" (p. 63). The novel itself provides no answer. Men about to lay down their lives can only dedicate their actions "to the record," and as for any reason why events turn out as they do, the novel offers only a circular argument—because that's the way people are. In *The Sirens of Titan* (1959), man's quest for meaning in his universe and for purpose in his existence undergoes a more direct exploration. Again the future provides the setting, but this time the actions, like the questions probed, are cosmic. In this, the most science fictional of all Vonnegut's novels, travel in space and time serves to explore the existential "whys" only touched on in *Player Piano*. But the new dimensions of space and time do more than serve Vonnegut's shift of emphasis beyond the immediate social issues—they provide an appropriate context for his assertions that the answers to man's questions exist not in the outer realms that science may help him explore, but within man himself.

Most fantasy fiction, be it of time travel, of space travel, or of fabulous voyages on this planet in the writer's own time, really only brings us to the mirror. It may even take us through the mirror. Yet its purpose remains that of showing us the reality of the writer's own time and society. He may construct an inverted image of that reality, and he may present reality by way of surrealism, but basically, no matter how devious and complex the travels of the protagonist, the writer travels in a straight line. If he takes us back into the past, he presents it with emphasis on the origins and development of those aspects of the present which concern him most. Similarly, his construction of the future usually involves projecting certain aspects of the present along straight lines to the point of their logical conclusions. Thus no matter how bizarre or fantastic a future we may be shown, we can trace it back to the present. This is one of our pleasures in such literature. We anticipate the fantastic, the futuristic, but we also enjoy that mental activity which goes on as we keep running back along those lines to the present, saying, "Yes, yes, that's right, that follows." Being shown some consequences of *all* men being someday replaced by machines makes us see afresh our own society in which *some* men are so displaced. This straight-line projection from the present makes the fantastic future nevertheless recognizable and gives it plausibility. That is why that Harvard student who seems destined to be quoted as long as Vonnegut is discussed could write, "The whole idea is funny because we know it could happen." In fact, however, while the future *could* resemble such direct extensions of the present, it might equally well not. Present developments in automation, for example, might suggest the ultimate redundancy of men. On the other hand, one might project from the SST cancellation and the ecological obsession to a point in time where machines are totally rejected. More probably, neither course would be followed. What so often makes past fiction about the future look quaint is the fact that human beings have seldom followed the predicted, straight-line courses.

Something else which makes the process of tracing back the lines of the future (or of the otherwise fantastic) to the reality of the present stems from the fact that fantasy writing is often satiric. One of the reader's joys in satire comes from "knowing where the ball is." We can indulge the thought that the objects of the satire, those less perceptive than ourselves, and those opposed to the view we enjoy in the satire, may not see through the technique, while we share with the satirist the knowledge of what is really intended. In reading science fiction we can enjoy tracing the projection of the present in the future world shown and recognizing an at least potential consequence of present social behavior to which its practitioners seem blind.

Much of Vonnegut's writing seems to build on just such straight-line projection of aspects of the present. George Orwell, Aldous Huxley and H. G. Wells did the same in writing of the future; Jonathan Swift, Mark Twain and Evelyn Waugh followed this formula in their geographic journeyings. As already suggested, the straight line may not be the surest course to a future point, but then the writer is generally not primarily concerned with the future as he has portrayed it, only with a more general future which he feels will be bad unless we make changes now. *Now* is essentially his first concern. Science fiction is generally more descriptive than predictive. Even as a technique for exposing the present, however, the logically projected future has its limitations. One of its greatest drawbacks may be the very thing which makes it so appealing—its seeming logic. For that logic may actually be simply a vehicle for emotion, and the apparent inevitability a cloak for sentiment or prejudice. Such visions of the future are usually based on scaling-up aspects of the present—aspects selected emotionally or sentimentally. The "square's" vision of a future populated by a bomb-throwing, drug-addicted great-unwashed may derive from his emotional reaction to "today's youth." Comic or satiric portrayals of the future easily become exaggerations of emotionally or even prejudicially selective views of the complexity of the present. But more than that, seemingly logical straight-line projections can encourage us, can deceive us, into believing that positions held out of sentiment or emotion are logically supported or even rationally based. Vonnegut, incidentally, seems much aware of this danger when he repeatedly warns, as in *Cat's Cradle,* of seeming truths being lies.

Nevertheless, the straight-line projection can be valid if not necessarily true. The Peter Principle and Parkinson's Laws, for example, operate on just such seeming logic but remain as useful to the understanding of our society as the solemn laws of Malthus and Adam Smith. One might even argue that America's Indo-China policy fits the category. That policy was largely predicated on the straight-line Domino Theory—that if a foreign power went into Viet Nam it would inevitably go into Thailand, Laos and Cambodia, too. We did. The fantasy writer's vision can be seen as equally valid if not always presenting the whole truth. For example, in *Player Piano*, Vonnegut tells us of an industrial revolution which has taken place before the action of the story, in which workers have wrecked machines which had replaced them. He supports this by pointing backward to the eighteenth century Industrial Revolution, where workers also wrecked machinery. That workers did, in fact, wreck machines in a roughly parallel historical situation lends credence to the notion that they would in a hypothetical future one. But there is a more immediate validity. Vonnegut shows in this way not that we will necessarily face another era of machine smashing if we go on as we are, but that the conditions which could lead to such actions are extant or in the

60

making. Recent events at the British Ford Motor Company plants, where the incidence of industrial sabotage has been high—and has been attributed by a reputable English sociologist to emotions in the workers and to conditions surrounding them similar in essence if not degree to those depicted in *Player Piano*—illustrate the validity of Vonnegut's projection. So that while such fantasy worlds seldom pretend to represent true or complete pictures of present or future, they can intensify our awareness of aspects of what is and of what may well come. It is in this way that fantasy fiction takes us through the mirror, rather than simply showing us the reflection of reality.

In *The Sirens of Titan*, which follows the science fiction form more consistently than any of Vonnegut's other novels and which goes farthest into the future, there is very little emphasis on prediction. In fact, the novel remains less concerned with social commentary be it in past, present or future, than with the timeless question of man's relationship to his Universe and to his own inner being. One of the strengths of this novel, which might well be considered Vonnegut's best, is the success with which the science fiction technique is employed to those ends.

The Sirens of Titan begins with a reverse of *Player Piano's* nostalgia: a persona, speaking from a more remote future, tells us that this is the story of a less happy era falling between "the Second World War and the Third Great Depression." Then, he says, men did not know that the meaning of life was within themselves, they searched all creation for meaning but found only meaninglessness, they left inwardness unexplored, and they gave themselves over to "gimcrack religion." The narrator then slips into the present of this dark age.

Malachi Constant, richest man in America, tycoon and playboy, arrives at the Rumfoord estate on the summons of Beatrice Rumfoord. Her husband, Winston, and his dog, Kazak, have plunged into a chrono-synclastic infundibulum while taking Rumfoord's private spaceship to Mars. The infundibulum is a sort of gyre in time and space, within which all truths become known. One result of Rumfoord's entering it is that he materializes at various times and places in space at regular intervals. It is to his next expected materialization at the estate that Constant has been summoned.

Constant does not know why Rumfoord has requested his visit, but he goes partly because he finds his life empty and halfway expects some divine intervention to give it purpose. His name, he knows, means "faithful messenger," and he "pined for just one thing—a single message that was sufficiently dignified and important to merit his carrying it humbly between two points" (p. 17). Constant believes in his luck, and insists on repeating "somebody up there likes me," a motto which becomes ironic by the end of the novel.

Rumfoord materializes and tells Constant that he will marry Beatrice on Mars, will visit Mercury, then return to Earth before reaching Titan, where he will be reunited with Beatrice and their son Chrono. To lessen Constant's aversion to the prediction, Rumfoord tells him Titan has a perfect climate and the most beautiful women in the universe, showing a picture of three—from whom the book takes its title.

Beatrice and Constant both resist the prediction. Malachi sells his control of Galactic Spacecraft which owns *The Whale,* a spaceship left over from the days before the discovery of chrono-synclastic infundibula put an end to space travel, and the only apparent means to fulfilling the prophecy. Beatrice sells all to buy Galactic so that Constant cannot use *The Whale* to carry her off into space. The sale, and a riotous drunk during which he gives away oil wells, ruin Constant. He goes to a dingy hotel, formerly the haunt of his father who had made a fortune using a Gideon Bible as a code to stock buying, to read the letter his parent has left for him there. The letter says only that the father had found some men lucky, others not, and leaves one instruction: "What I want you to try and find out is, is there anything special going on or is it all just as crazy as it looked to me?" (p. 90).

At the hotel, two Martian agents talk Constant into

escaping the ruins of his empire by volunteering for service on Mars. The same agents, posing as financial advisors, kidnap Beatrice just as she has witnessed the launching of *The Whale* (now renamed *The Rumfoord*) and for the first time feels safe.

On Mars, Rumfoord has created a large army staffed with people decoyed from Earth and rendered virtually robots by means of antennae placed in their skulls. Constant has become a private in the army, working his way down through the ranks by way of seven operations to cleanse his memory and to stop him thinking. Known as "Unk" to other soldiers, he has forgotten his former identity completely. Under the control of his antenna, we see him carry out a military execution on a former friend—by strangling him. As he dies, the friend, Stony, tells Unk to look for what turns out to be a journal in which Unk has recorded all he knows about himself and affairs on Mars. Unk deserts and tries unsuccessfully to persuade his son Chrono and mate Bee—who is now teaching Schliemann breathing, a means of absorbing oxygen from pills while in hostile atmospheres—to join him.

At this point, Rumfoord reappears to tell Unk-Constant how he had seduced Bee in the spaceship from Earth to Mars, conceiving Chrono. The Martian armies leave for Earth for a sort of war to end all wars. Rumfoord's idea is that attack from space will unite all on Earth, and that annihilation of his small suicide force will turn people from war in revulsion. The war, in fact, does achieve this end, and also facilitates the birth of Rumfoord's new religion—the Church of God the Utterly Indifferent. Its motto reads: *"Take Care of the People, and God Almighty Will Take Care of Himself"* (p. 180).

Unk has no part in the invasion, however, being sent off to Mercury with another soldier named Boaz. Their spaceship alights at the bottom of a deep and complex cavern from which they can find no escape. The cavern is populated by harmoniums, luminous triangular creatures which draw energy from sound. Boaz comes to love them, and they him, as he feeds them on the energy of his own heartbeat and music from the spaceship's tape library.

63

After two years on Mercury, Unk receives a message from Rumfoord that he can escape by turning the spaceship upside down, since its sensors are in its lower surfaces. So while Boaz chooses to stay with the harmoniums, Unk sets out for Earth.

Unk is welcomed on Earth as "The Space Wanderer" whose coming is prophesied in the new religion. The people, all handicapped to make them equal—some carrying weights, others marring their beauty—welcome their new messiah at the Rumfoord estate, which forms the new Church's Mecca. There Unk says the confirming words the believers have awaited: "I was a victim of a series of accidents, as are we all." Bee and Chrono, who with other Martian survivors work as concessionaires at the estate, are unemotionally reunited with Unk. But the messiah's hour of glory is quickly reversed. Malachi Constant has served as the personification of evil for the new religion because of his grasping egocentrism and his belief in luck as divine favor—anathema to the believers in equality and divine indifference. Now Rumfoord identifies Unk as Malachi Constant, and demolishes Unk's last self-respect by revealing to him that he had killed his one true friend, Stony.

So the messiah is crucified—or, rather, sent off into space with Chrono and Bee. Their destination is Titan, where Rumfoord (as the infundibulum permits) inhabits a personal Taj Mahal in company with a Tralfamadorian named Salo. The latter is a robot from a planet where robots have taken over completely. He has helped Rumfoord carry out all his plans on Mars and Earth to help while away the few thousand years that he has been on Titan. Salo's mission, to carry a message to a planet on the opposite extreme of the universe from Tralfamadore, has been stalled for lack of replacement for a defective part of his spaceship. The Tralfamadorians have controlled all that has happened as a means for getting that part to Salo—even to Earth's great constructions, like Stonehenge, being simply for messages of reassurance. Even the "sirens" of Titan, those three lovely women of the photograph, turn out to be statues made by Salo. As

Constant and family arrive, Rumfoord is about to depart the galaxy because a storm of sunspots has disturbed his infundibulum. Before he departs, he begs Salo to reveal the message he is carrying to prove his friendship. All Salo's "instincts"— or programming—are set against his revealing his message, and he refuses. Rumfoord cruelly accuses Salo of not being a friend, then disappears. Too late, Salo changes his mind and reveals the message. It reads simply: "Greetings." Overwrought by the fear that he has failed his friend and proved "inhuman," the robot self-destructs.

Constant, Bee and Chrono live out their lives on Titan. Bee dies having learned that being used is better than being of no use to anyone. Chrono, whose lucky piece has turned out to be the spare part Salo awaits, goes to live with Titan's giant bluebirds, and last appears to thank his parents for the gift of life. Constant learns to love Bee before she dies—and also reconstructs Salo. The Tralfamadorian, now that he has his replacement part, decides to resume his mission, and gives Constant a lift to Earth. There the space wanderer dies waiting for a bus, with visions of a paradise where he is reunited with Stony— all posthypnotic suggestion planted by Salo.

While the events portrayed in *The Sirens of Titan* are scattered around the universe, reflecting the protagonist's aimless but directed wanderings, the narrative development of the story remains straightforward. There are far fewer digressions, subplots and simultaneous developments to keep track of than in *Player Piano*, a fact which helps to make the second novel smoother reading. *Player Piano* has unity of place, narrows itself to the depiction of a particular society and to more immediate social and moral problems, yet *The Sirens of Titan*, for all its wanderings, futurity, and concern with larger, abstract questions, transmits a greater sense of direction and concreteness. Rather surprising, too, is the fact that this novel with its science fiction orientation, with its robots and near-robot humans, and with its several central characters who are intentionally presented as being rather cold-hearted, generates more human warmth than *Player Piano* which is directly concerned with the agonies of exploring and following conscience, emotion and love. Three possible explanations for this phenomenon present themselves: first, Vonnegut's skill has grown in the intervening seven years; second, the science fiction mode affords the author more detachment, and he is less didactic in this work; third, the positive forces, particularly love, carry more weight.

Many of the same formulae, however, operate in both novels. Malachi Constant corresponds to Paul Proteus as a protagonist who feels uncertain and vaguely dissatisfied with his life, and who, partly through resistance to manipulation by others and partly out of loyalty to a friend, undergoes a considerable change of values. Each emerges somewhat battered, rather disillusioned but with some beliefs to affirm, and a stronger, more honest man. Aspects of the future derive directly from the present, frequently with the purpose of satirizing and making moral judgment upon our society. There is an outside observer of human affairs in each novel, but this time from the reverse perspective: Salo is a robot from a vastly more advanced society. (Ironically, however, Salo displays more "human" feeling than any other character, and his judgments on human behavior often resemble the Shah's.) One can even see parallels between Lasher and Rumfoord, each creating with some cynicism a new religion for the times and making a messiah of the protagonist. Some lesser repeated motifs include the depiction of sex as unsatisfying, and satires of the presidency and the army. One topic which remains almost in the background in *Player Piano* becomes central in *The Sirens of Titan*— that is the question of the meaning of existence. In *Player Piano*, Berringer asks "why did it have to happen?" when Checker Charley burns up, Homesteaders bemusedly insist men must be meant for something, and the Shah asks some fundamental questions about the meaning of the new American Utopia. But the emphasis remains on the social implications of the question. In *The Sirens of Titan*, the question arises in broader philosophical terms.

That narrator who opens the story, speaking as if to an audience of the future, says that this is an account of life when men searched outside of themselves, going into space only to find what they had found on Earth—"a nightmare of meaninglessness without end" (p. 8). Inwardness, the soul—which he says everyone now recognizes as the source of meaning—remained unexplored. Indeed, at the outset of the story, signs of the search for meaning from without abound. Rumfoord has been lost—for most of the time, anyway—on a jaunt to Mars. Crowds throng around his estate at his materialization as if waiting for a sign. They press in on Malachi hysterically as he leaves. " 'We've got a right to know what's going on!' " one woman cries.

> The riot, then, was an exercise in science and theology—a seeking after clues by the living as to what life was all about (p. 44).

Constant himself "pines" for a message to carry that will give his life meaning and purpose. His father, whose financial wizardry convinces onlookers that he, if anybody, must know what is going on, leaves Malachi one last assignment:

> *What I want you to try and find out is, is there anything special going on, or is it all just as crazy as it looked to me?* (p. 90)

The Reverend Bobby Denton, the evangelist who presumably qualifies as a practitioner of one of the "gimcrack religions" alluded to, denies the need for space travel, but argues against it using the metaphor of Earth as a spaceship, and by insisting that all men need to know can be satisfied in adherence to the Bible. Even Beatrice, who hates and resists Rumfoord's prophecy that she will travel in space and be mated with Constant, begs her husband for knowledge of what will happen to her.

The intense need for meaning among these people leads to their supplying meaning for what may be only coincidence or chance. As Shakespeare's Duke Theseus says,

67

> "Such tricks hath strong imagination
> That if it would but apprehend some joy,
> It comprehends some bringer of that joy"
> —*A Midsummer Night's Dream,* V-i-18-20.

Thus, Constant explains his luck by saying, "Somebody up there likes me," his father clings superstitiously to his Gideon Bible-derived stock-buying scheme, and Chrono treasures the "good luck piece" (on the face of it no more than a bit of scrap metal) which he feels distinguishes him. Within the novel, Rumfoord sets out to convince the people, Constant in particular, of the meaninglessness of life. His entry into the chrono-synclastic infundibulum, where so many truths and times become knowable to him, provides a revelation: "When I ran my spaceship into the chrono-synclastic infundibulum, it came to me in a flash that everything that ever has been always will be, and everything that ever will be always has been" (pp. 25-6). His conception of the universe as operating arbitrarily according to preordained patterns, with complete disregard for man, leads Rumfoord to attempt his education of Constant and Beatrice, and to substitute for the "gimcrack religions" his Church of God the Utterly Indifferent. Similarly, though with less apparent cynicism, the author presents a comparable view in his portrayal of an absurd universe.

Rumfoord's vision of a universe in which the future is fixed proves unpopular with all the major characters. Vonnegut seems to confirm the obvious truth that while people often want to know the future—as if assuming that future already laid out—they find the notion of being unable to change what they do not like repugnant. Even Rumfoord himself finds the inevitability of things to come depressing. When his wife wants him to use his vision to give her stock market tips to escape her becoming, as she puts it, "a space whore for Malachi Constant," Rumfoord wearily argues the futility of his doing so. Admittedly he can see "the whole roller-coaster" she is on, and could tell her of all the dangers, but that would not help her: " 'Because you'd *still* have to take the roller-coaster ride,' said Rumfoord. 'I didn't design the roller-coaster, I don't own it, and I don't say who rides and who doesn't. I just know what it's shaped like'" (p. 58). Strong-willed woman that she is, Beatrice sets out to resist. Not liking what the ride promises, she decides not to get on it. But her very resistance becomes part of the inevitable scheme —the financial advisors who assist her plan to remain on Earth turn out to be the Martian agents sent to kidnap her. The little she has been given to see of the future proves only a handicap, destroying what pleasure she might find in the present and actually leading her to play into the hands of the inevitable. In her defense, it should be remembered that "in one of the few known instances of Winston Niles Rumfoord's having told a lie" (p. 58), she is intentionally deceived into believing she will go to Mars on the spaceship *The Whale*. She accordingly directs her defense against the wrong quarter.

For Malachi Constant, too, Rumfoord's revelations prove both disturbing and unhelpful. Like Beatrice, he assists the inevitable by the dissolution of his financial empire and by turning himself over to Martian agents. There is a difference in the behavior of the two, however: Beatrice resists single-mindedly, Malachi with some ambivalence. While he also starts by making financial moves to thwart the prophecy, he appears to feel both resigned and in a way attracted to what has been predicted for him. As he leaves his first interview with Rumfoord, he senses that something was indeed "looking out for him," saving him for a bizarre series of space journeys and, from all he can tell, a lonely death on Titan. The would-be messenger sees some potential for purpose in his journeyings, and the notion of exterior control touches a familiar chord in this man who has always insisted, "somebody up there likes me." Hence his resignation. When those shady agents offer him employment on Mars, he accepts partly to escape an untenable situation on Earth, but partly with the same resignation that had led to his disastrous drunken orgy.

Resistance to the lot assigned by "fates" or "something up there" remains futile throughout but can at least improve the man. Constant's most admirable resistance occurs during his service on Mars. There he rebels against being turned into a mindless robot by trying to remember, trying to think, keeping a journal and sustaining as long as he can his alliance with Stony. The Martian camp represents, of course, a bizarre travesty of the human condition on Earth. Rumfoord is its unseen and dimly comprehended god. Meaningless lives are controlled toward absurd deaths. Thought and reflection are painful, conformity and acquiescence easy. Yet men continue to question, to think, to search for meaning. In terms of its achievement, the resistance of Constant-Unk proves futile. He fails in his attempt to escape with his family, he murders his one true friend, and as the returning "Space Wanderer" he serves out his appointed role as messiah and sacrifice. Yet while not changing the course of events, his resistance does change the nature of what happens. He refuses to become merely a robot, he struggles to assert some meaningful self-identity in an incoherent universe, he comes to believe in the value of friendship and he learns to love.

Constant's conversion, then, involves a greater change than does that of Proteus in *Player Piano*. Initially he appears as a self-centered, thoughtless, dissolute playboy, surfeited in drugs, alcohol, women and luxury. By the end he has become modest, self-reliant, loving and loyal. The change comes through much suffering. On Mars, for instance, he undergoes no fewer than seven operations to "cleanse his memory." He struggles to remember, to fit together what he knows, even though the antenna sends intense pains through his head whenever he reflects. Apart from his sufferings in Rumfoord's armies, Constant has to face the rejections of his family, two years in the caves of Mercury, the discovery that he has killed the one man he has really cared for, being reviled by the same crowds who had bewilderingly welcomed him as a messiah, and again space exile within hours of returning to his native planet. Yet he is unembittered at the end. When—speaking of drains, ironically—Beatrice tells him to do "whatever needs to be done," he can reply with some humor,

70

" 'That's the story of my life' " (p. 310). Perhaps he shares the conclusion Beatrice, who has been so embittered by Rumfoord's use of her, reaches just before she dies: " 'The worst thing that could possibly happen to anybody,' she said, 'would be to not be used for anything by anybody' " (p. 310). He spends his last days on Titan caring for (and eventually burying) Beatrice, and keeping up the former Rumfoord palace for whoever might come there next. He loves his son, who has left to join the giant bluebirds, as best he can from a distance by tending the shrines Chrono builds. Above all, he has learned to love, as he tells Salo after Beatrice's death: " 'It took us that long to realize that a purpose of human life, no matter who is controlling it, is to love whoever is around to be loved' " (p. 313).

The struggles of Beatrice and Constant to contend with Rumfoord's prophecies and with being used or controlled represent two versions of living with a known future and an absence of free will. Beatrice knows what will happen in a general way, but is misinformed about how. For the most part she regards Rumfoord as directly responsible for her manipulation. Constant knows a little more about what will happen and how, and learns that control does not stop with Rumfoord. A third version of the pattern occurs in the case of Rumfoord himself. Rumfoord can see "the whole roller-coaster ride," and even knows that all his actions are shaped ultimately by the Tralfamadorians. The puppeteer is himself a puppet. The crowds on Earth have sought some clue to the meaning of life and to what the future holds: here we have three variations on what can happen when man does have at least a glimmering of his future and of its meaning. Beatrice and Constant find that knowing the future helps little if at all, and discover that there is no comprehensible meaning to the Universe. Knowing the future only heightens their awareness of their lack of free will and their inability to determine their own fates, while the only purpose they have found is their use to satisfy the whims of Rumfoord and to help convey something like a beer-can opener to Titan. What they *do* learn, in effect, is that their expectations have been wrong. By the end neither feels so offended by lack of free will, by being used, or by not knowing the future. But each has learned something about being in that condition. They have, as the opening of the novel implies all men must, found meaning by turning inward rather than by searching for it outside themselves.

Whether Rumfoord achieves a comparable adjustment proves less easy to assess. At times he appears to enjoy his role as bringer of bad tidings and as manipulator, and smiles with the detached amusement of a super-human at the discomfiture his prophecies cause his wife and Constant. We may forgive his early distaste for these two, but his taunting of Constant while trapped on Mercury and on his return as "The Space Wanderer" seems too cold-blooded. His plan to use the Martians to bring the peoples of Earth to unity and to a final recognition of the excesses of war is another troubling episode. Vonnegut's handling of it is partly comic and in part bitter satire—obviously it should not be read solemnly even though it makes some serious observations. But in terms of its impact on Rumfoord's characterization it suggests a man who enjoys manipulating, who likes to use the rod to assist his teaching, and who is frighteningly devoid of compassion. His ends are admirable, but his means remain deplorable. Much the same can be said of his exploitation of Constant as Unk the messiah and Malachi the scapegoat, and of his calculated callousness toward the loyal Salo.

Of course, Rumfoord is in a rum situation, condemned to apparently eternal floating in space, materializing now on this planet, now on that, and subject to nausea and partial atomization whenever there are sunspots. His knowledge of the future proves the most burdensome of all, since it is the most complete. He knows he will be denied even the comfort of a normal human death on Earth, that his wife will be seduced by a man he despises (though that seems to trouble him little), and that that man will father the son he cannot and find at the end the love he is forever denied. This knowledge and the glimpses we have of the child "Skip" may tend to soften our judgment. Yet we see enough of his early life, particularly through Beatrice's eyes, to suspect that his post-chrono-synclastic infundibulum condition only exaggerates what he always has been. His impotence remains as a physical manifestation of his incapacity to love.

Perhaps Rumfoord is entitled to feel the most terribly manipulated of all the characters, not just for what he has been condemned to live through and foreknow, but also for what he must do to others. Salo fears that if Rumfoord knew he was being used by the Tralfamadorians it would end their friendship, and indeed that knowledge does cause a strain.

> "Tralfamadore," said Rumfoord bitterly, "reached into the Solar System, picked me up, and used me like a handy-dandy potato peeler!" (p. 285)

Ironically, the manipulator of the Martians finds this intolerable. " 'Nobody likes to think he's being used' " (p. 285), he says. Rumfoord has cause to be cynical. But his cynicism, his pose of aloof, aristocratic, even super-human detachment, is what makes him so unsympathetic a character. In bringing Constant and Beatrice to aware-ness, and in harmonizing the people of Earth, he seldom appears less than contemptuous of them. It seems entirely appropriate that his companion in space is a dog from whom he can command obedience and respect. Constant, on his way to Titan, can call the Universe a junkyard where all the bargains are overpriced and wired to dyna-mite, and draw the assent of his family. Yet even after that all three come to some affirmative view of life. Rum-foord never does. We last see him launching into a coldly destructive argument with Salo, demanding that the latter reveal the secret message he carries. Unlike Beatrice and Constant, he remains devoid of love, resentful of being used and, most ironically, still looking for an answer "outside."

Rumfoord's role as cynical prophet and manipulator, however, serves as a buffer for the author. Without the presence of a spokesman for the inevitability of events, the absence of human free will, the lack of meaning in the Universe, and the meaner aspects of human behavior, this cynicism might accrue to the author himself and change the tone of the novel. In *Player Piano* there is no such persona who appears directly responsible for turning men into machines, for example, and if what happens seems bleak or negative we take it as part of the vision of the author. In *The Sirens of Titan,* the bleaker and more negative aspects in the view of the Universe presented are associated with (and *appear* often to be the responsibilities of) Rumfoord, while the total vision includes affirmative possibilities as well. Consequently the novel's emphasis falls not on asserting the absurdity of existence, but upon the possibilities of giving life in an absurd Universe some meaning, dignity, and human warmth. This frame of reference is stressed by the fact that Rumfoord, rather than being lionized for his recognition of the nature of existence, is rejected for his failure to arrive at a genuinely human response to it, ultimately being cast out of the Solar System without even his dog.

The question of free will, so troublesome to the characters in this novel, becomes something of a problem to the reader, too, in the case of Rumfoord. We are led to believe that Rumfoord's plunge into the chrono-synclastic infundibulum marks the first step in a Tralfamadorian scheme to transport the needed replacement part (Chrono's good-luck piece) to Salo on Titan. Some question remains about how much free will he retains within this general framework of inevitability. We may be tempted to share the judgment of Beatrice that while Tralfamadorians shape events on Earth, those who have served Tralfamadorian interests have done so in "highly personalized ways" which go beyond the influence of outside agents (p. 309). It could be argued that the *way* the man carries out the inevitable plan is part of the inevitability, part of the "everything that ever was always will be, and everything that ever will be always was." But if that explains Rumfoord's actions, it also explains away, in a sense, the virtue of Constant's learning to love, Salo's compassion, Chrono's discovery of joy in life, or anything else affirmative. While such a scheme would confirm with terrible consistency the meaninglessness of the Universe, it would also make the murders in the narrative no better and no worse than the hard-won love—and that, surely, is more than Vonnegut wants to convey. Perhaps we should conclude that "T'were to consider too curiously, to consider so"—at least in a comically conceived work of science fiction.

What we can consider is that Vonnegut wants to explore some of the consequences of a modern view of time not simply as a series of chronologically passing moments but of coexistent tenses, the sort of thing T. S. Eliot postulates in the opening of *Burnt Norton*:

> Time present and time past
> Are both perhaps present in time future,
> And time future contained in time past.

Vonnegut also exposes the hypocrisy involved in wanting to know the future, which essentially assumes inevitability, while retaining the free will to change what one does not like. Beyond this the novel tests the scope of man's free will simply in the face of larger forces or, more broadly, within the context of an absurd Universe. For one thing, the novel suggests that free will implies the presence of meaning, even of some universal power that can observe the actions and respond to the wishes of man, and which can adjust the course of the future. Salo's statues on Titan are inspired by his watching humans behaving according to these assumptions: "The Earthlings behaved at all times as though there were a big eye in the sky—as though that big eye were ravenous for entertainment" (p. 276). The "big eye," of course, often amounts ultimately to a version of God. Bobby Denton's sermon, for example, builds on the premise that if people please his particular "big eye in the sky" they will be well taken care of. It is precisely this sort of assumption that Rumfoord's "Church of God the Utterly Indifferent" sets out to counter. Its creed is expressed in the words of Constant on his return to Earth:

> I WAS A VICTIM OF A SERIES OF ACCIDENTS, AS
> ARE WE ALL. (p. 229)

This creed answers the motto placed on a billboard by
the earlier "gimcrack religions":

> LET'S TAKE A FRIEND TO THE CHURCH OF *OUR*
> CHOICE ON SUNDAY! (p. 44, italics added.)

One episode which bears directly on freedom of choice
and how to adapt to a meaningless Universe centers
around the Martian soldier, Boaz. As one of the actual
commanders of the army, though appearing to be only a
menial private, Boaz carries a control box which sends
impulses to the antennae implanted in the heads of Rumfoord's human robots. Like other commanders, Boaz has
a good deal of freedom—from normal military restrictions
and to use his powers for his own entertainment: "Boaz
had no antenna in his own skull. As free as it wanted to
be—that's how free the free will of Boaz was" (p. 116).
Of course, this observation proves ironic. Boaz's lack of
imagination and experience limits how much free will he
even wants, as does his total situation on Mars. In a
sense, his free will extends little further than his control
box, and once Unk-Constant removes that, Boaz's scope
diminishes.

During the long imprisonment in the caverns of Mercury, the former tormentor of his barrack-mates becomes
a much more sympathetic character. His reaction to the
situation contrasts with Constant's. Unk regards their
entombment as another sign that his environment is
either "malevolent or cruelly mismanaged," and struggles against it with "passive resistance and open displays
of contempt" (p. 200). He roams the caverns, following
the tracks of Rumfoord and Kazak, like an aging savage.
Boaz, on the other hand, feeds on the need and "love" of
the harmoniums, prospers physically and emotionally. He
provides a classic example of "making the best of things,"
establishing a daily ritual, keeping himself busy and
organized. Since they are being tested by something beyond
his comprehension, Boaz reasons, "all I can do is be
friendly and keep calm and try and have a nice time till

it's over" (p. 202). Once escape becomes possible, he elects to stay with his harmoniums on Mercury. The harmoniums, translucent, skate-like creatures which feed on sound vibrations, have become the focus of Boaz's life. He feeds them on his own heartbeat and on tape-recorded music, loving them and assuming they love him. When they form patterns which spell out "BOAZ, DON'T GO!" he is unable to resist, even when he recognizes it may be a trick. (Rumfoord uses the harmoniums to spell out messages to Unk.) " 'I found me a place where I can do good without doing any harm. . . ,' " he says. " 'I found me a home' " (p. 214).

Commendable though Boaz's adjustment and intentions may be in many ways, they are undercut. The "love" of the harmoniums flatters him, and at a moment when he prides himself on his role his unattended tape-recorder kills hundreds of creatures. The harmless harmoniums with their sweet but entirely automatic message transmissions—

"Here I am, here I am, here I am."
"So glad you are, so glad you are, so glad you are." (p. 186)

—have an obvious appeal. But it represents an appeal to regression, to infantile visions of sweetness and light. Boaz's choice of the caves over "freedom" is a rather obvious return-to-the-womb impulse, a regression underlined by his childlike ritual of telling himself, "You're a good boy, Boaz. . . You go to sleep now" (p. 214). He escapes the futile fury and resistance of Unk, but his adjustment becomes merely submission. To see the danger of such a pattern we have only to look back at Boaz on Mars—adjusted and submissive, playing with his robot soldiers.

So the apparent conversion of Boaz turns out to be less than it promises. It fluctuates between being genuinely touching and simply sentimental, with the ironic undercutting perhaps finally swaying the balance. Boaz *is* tricked —Rumfoord wants Constant to go on alone. The sentiment is in Boaz himself more than in Vonnegut's handling of the passage. And, after all, Boaz has found a way to love and does benefit the harmoniums, even if the love becomes flawed and the benefit qualified. Sentiment remains, of course, as indeed it must at this point. It is necessary to contrast with the coldness of the loveless world of Mars and with Constant's indignant resistance, and it is necessary to emphasize the fallible warmth of human emotions. Sentiment frequently emerges in Vonnegut where he contrasts the human with the machine or machine-like. Usually he shows that he recognizes it for what it is—certainly more often in *The Sirens of Titan* than in *Player Piano*. He undercuts it with irony in such a way as to give rise to that peculiarly poignant kind of humor which becomes a characteristic of his work. We see this effect again in the portrayal of that persevering Tralfamadorian messager, Salo.

Tralfamadore, we are told, was once populated by creatures resembling humans in that they were preoccupied with discovering their purpose, but (much as in *Player Piano*) they always found any purpose too low and invented a machine for it. The machines were eventually set to finding out the purpose of the creatures, reporting that there was none. Exasperated by purposelessness, the creatures fought—with the aid of machines, who soon wiped out all of the creatures. Hence Tralfamadore's four-million year old machine civilization. Salo has been sent to carry a message to the opposite side of the Universe, but for 200,000 years has been stranded on Titan, one of the nine moons of Saturn. Here he meets Rumfoord, whom he assists with the necessary technology for the Martian army plan. Salo spends much of his time observing humans on Earth, and seems to believe he has developed many of his "emotions" from doing so, although the indications are that the Tralfamadorians are affectionate and humorous types anyway. For example, their message to the other end of the Universe is simply "Greetings," and their signals to the long-stranded Salo are breezily cheerful—" 'You will be on your way before you know it' " (p. 271).

Salo represents another variation on the "keeping going

in the face of the absurd" theme. His long sojourn on Titan roughly parallels that of Constant and Boaz on Mars. He spends his time cultivating flowers, sculpting, watching the activities on Earth and, in the later years, building his friendship with Rumfoord. To the extent that he makes the best of a trying situation he resembles Boaz; his refusal to become embittered or to reject the only opportunities for love and friendship available contrasts with Constant's attitudes. But in the end these alignments reverse. Rumfoord's callous rejection of Salo, his taunting of the sensitive machine for being inhuman, devastate the Tralfamadorian much as the news that he has killed Stony demoralizes Constant. When Rumfoord insists that the one way Salo can prove he is not merely a machine would be by exposing the message he has been "programmed" to keep secret, the robot, after much torment, reveals it. That message—"Greetings"—makes Salo as much a messenger of no real consequence as "The Space Wanderer" himself has been.

Having lost his friend, and feeling purposeless and used, Salo "commits suicide" by disassembling himself. At this point he has been brought to the point of total negation, much as Constant has at the same moment. On Titan, Constant goes through a ritualistic denial of life:

"I resign," said Constant.
"I withdraw," said Constant.
"I quit," said Constant. (p. 290)

Constant's conception of life at this time is emphasized in his encounter with the echo which reiterates the last word of his questions.

"Life?" said the echo.
"It's an echo," said Beatrice.
"I know it's an echo," said Constant. (p. 291)

The perhaps too neat ambiguity makes the point: life for Constant is an echo—everything that ever has been always will be, and everything that ever will be always has been. Reaching this point of resignation through the full recognition of the meaninglessness of the universe appears, however, to be a necessary step in coming to terms with that condition. Only after Constant has been reduced to this state, brought to this realization after years of resisting and trying to find meaning outside of himself, does it become possible for him to find peace within, love for those around him, and purpose in actions which serve those others. Likewise Salo, reassembled by Constant, chooses to come to life again and, with his ship repaired, resume his journey. " 'Anybody who has traveled this far on a fool's errand,' said Salo, 'has no choice but to uphold the honor of fools by completing the errand' " (p. 313).

There is sentimentality, of course, in the depiction of this lovable tangerine of a Tralfamadorian, but in this particular context of comic science fiction it seems far more acceptable than, say, that which surrounds the characterization of Finnerty in the greater social-realism of *Player Piano*. The comedy, and frequent irony, too, counters it just enough to preserve balance in the perspective of the narration, while at the level of the world within the fiction, some sentiment is what we hope to find in these cold recesses of time and space. Salo seems to have the right answer, for example, when he tells Rumfoord that he lives "punctually"—that is, one moment at a time—and that he would rather see the colors at the end of the spectrum than know the future. When he wishes Constant "Good luck," and Constant tells him that the expression is no longer approved "down here" in the world of God the Utterly Indifferent, Salo winks and says, " 'I'm not *from* down here' " (p. 317). We approve this, as we approve the posthypnotic dream with which he leaves Constant to meet death. When in that dream Stony tells Constant that somebody up there likes him, we know the deception is at least partially true—Salo does like him. In all of this Vonnegut comes close to the sentimentality he displays in his short story ("Epicac") of the computer that falls in love with a girl and commits suicide, but this time he has a more adequate supporting context. Salo's actions roughly parallel the affirmative turn in Constant's life, and become part of the thematic assertion of the purpose and meaning in loving whatever is around to be loved with which the book ends.

Whatever our sternest critical judgments might be as to whether the sentiment in the portrayal of Salo is justified, balanced by ironic undercutting, or simply excessive, we are likely to welcome it at least in a subjective, emotional way. Salo emphasizes in the ending an element of "human" warmth and affection which seems to have had only limited and tenuous existence earlier in the book. Even so, there is more of it in *The Sirens of Titan* than in *Player Piano*, or in most of the later novels. In *The Sirens of Titan*, the science fiction mode invokes as a given condition the cold indifference of the Universe and works toward the assertion of human feeling. That, along with the more positive affirmations the novel makes, explains much of the appeal of the story.

The Sirens of Titan offers many of the attractions we have come to expect of Vonnegut—social satire, topical commentary, comedy, disillusionment with middle-class norms, a delight in the preposterous, and so on. Science fiction allows his inventiveness full rein, with chronosynclastic infundibula, the Universal Will to Become, harmoniums, Tralfamadore and its government by "hypnotic anarchy," Martian invasion and antennae-controlled legions. The Martian army, with its remote-controlled human automatons marching to the antennae-induced chant of *"rented a tent, a tent, a tent,"* takes the parody of military mindlessness one stage further than that in *Player Piano*. To this pitiful rag-tag of outcasts, we are told, goes "the privilege of being the first army that ever died in a good cause" (p. 164). The war itself yields more strong satire—the Earth's massive over-response leaves its skies orange for a year and a half, the moon uninhabitable for ten million years. There is the grim comedy of Martians with ancient rifles facing atomic weaponry. In America civilians, including old women, delight in butchering the hapless Martians, and one mayor brashly calls for more to be sent—subsequently becoming a U.S. Senator. A Martian commander, called upon to surrender in a hopeless situation, defiantly answers, "Nuts!"

The satire of religions also goes somewhat further than in *Player Piano*. The portrayal of the evangelist Bobby Denton seems a fairly traditional handling of a stock target, though amusingly done. But with Rumfoord's "Church of God the Utterly Indifferent" the satire expands. As mentioned earlier, Rumfoord resembles Lasher in being a cynic who believes that people want circuses, and who will give them a messiah and lies along with truths to bring them to his desired end. To crown his efforts to make people believe in the indifference of the Universe, the apathy of God, and the need for brotherly love, Rumfoord takes his Space Wanderer through a parody of New Testament events, from glorious acclamation to the sermon of the panorama to rejection and expulsion into space. Of course, Rumfoord's new religion uses all the television hoopla and plastic Malachis of the grimcrack religion it replaces. One aspect of it which seems a little more original than others is the concept of equalizing handicaps. Some people carry weights to counter physical advantages, others wear glasses which spoil excellent eyesight, and a dark young man of "predaceous sex appeal" is handicapped with a wife nauseated by sex. Beautiful women have "annihilated that unfair advantage with frumpish clothes, bad posture, chewing gum, and a ghoulish use of cosmetics" p. 224). All of this makes people happy because nobody takes advantage of others, we are told. (The system of handicaps to eliminate unfair advantages is satirized further in the short story, "Harrison Bergeron.") Vonnegut has been accused sometimes of playing to his young followers, but in his debunking of egalitarian dreams the opposite might be true, since competition and shining over others are unpopular with this audience.

What might appeal to the youth audience, or the general stereotypes of it, is the recurrent attraction of dropping out. Generally speaking, the impulse to resignation does not win approval in the novel. Boaz's dream of doing good without doing any harm, beautiful though it may sound, remains regressive and partly self-deluding. Constant and Salo both "quit," but come back to soldier on, helping and loving where they can. Chrono's joining the giant bluebirds probably represents the most persuasive instance. Even Salo sees the appeal of it. " 'Good for him!' " he says. " 'I'd join them, if they'd have me' " (p. 314). From being a dishearteningly aggressive, cynical and unfeeling boy, Chrono comes to align himself with the most beautiful creatures available and to appreciate the gift of life. In the circumstances he makes perhaps the best choice possible. His election to stay with the bluebirds differs from Boaz's opting for the harmoniums in being an embracing of life rather than a retreat from it, a joining-with rather than the assumption of a god-role. Chrono's appalling childhood has left him still able to praise, as he does in his gratitude to his parents and in his shrines, and that in the circumstances is no small wonder. The final answer to opting out derives from the fact that Salo elects to go on with his mission knowing it absurd, and that Constant—like Prospero leaving his magical island, to go back to his own kind—chooses to return to the Earth that has treated him so badly.

Once again comedy contributes substantially to the appeal of this novel. Possibly the best comic passage is that which describes the Tralfamadorians' use of Earth civilizations and their buildings to convey messages to Salo. The ironic propriety of the messages to the buildings which spell them out is excellent:

Stonehenge: " 'Replacement part being rushed with all possible speed.' "
The Great Wall of China: " 'Be patient. We haven't forgotten about you.' "
The Golden House of Nero: " 'We are doing the best we can.' "
The Kremlin: " 'You will be on your way before you know it.' "
The Palace of the League of Nations: " 'Pack up your things and be ready to leave on short notice'." (pp. 271-2)

At other times Vonnegut makes use of homespun comic idioms and slapstick. There is the reaction of the shameless blonde who marries Constant believing him a multimillionaire: "Now I find out you haven't got a pot to piss in or a window to throw it out of' " (p. 62). Or Malachi himself, having discovered he has frittered away a financial empire in a succession of blunders, pleading, " 'A guy is entitled to a mistake now and then' " (p. 71). Also typical is the use of the riddle about the man locked in a room with only a bed and a calendar. He survives by eating the dates from the calendar and drinking the water from the springs of the bed (p. 72). Another characteristic element of the comic tone is the delight in the preposterous: Noel Constant making a fortune investing in companies whose initials fit the first sentence of Genesis, the Martian invasion, the infundibula, the massive Tralfamadorian effort to convey a single dot across the Universe.

The comedy has a major part in setting the tone of *The Sirens of Titan,* and while the comic devices resemble those seen in *Player Piano* and elsewhere they make a slightly different total impact. Overall, the humor in this novel seems less dark. There is less of the brand of humor which Joyce Cary described as that typical of a soldier in the trenches about to go "over the top" on a suicidal mission. We find more open laughter, less of the rather cynical, bitter, hurt chuckling of *Player Piano.* That, combined with the affirmative possibilities in the novel and the greater objective detachment Vonnegut achieves through the expanded use of the science fiction form, gives *The Sirens of Titan* a more immediately appealing tone than its predecessor. This is not to argue that the later book rates higher simply because it seems more cheerful, or that it presents a Pollyanna vision of the future. *The Sirens of Titan* remains a carefully balanced novel, with much of its humor of a distinctly painful variety, its triumphs frequently undercut, and its affirmations set in a frightening context. To be lulled by the warmer qualities of the story into disregarding its vision of an Absurd Universe would be for the reader himself to succumb to the sirens of Titan.

Ultimately, the real sirens of Titan are not those peerless beauties offering total fulfillment on a paradisical planet of perfect climate. They actually have little to do with what happens to Constant. He is led to Titan by the machinations of Rumfoord, and beyond that by the schemes of the Tralfamadorians, and beyond that—what? Perhaps only the meaningless, arbitrary workings of the Universe. In making the Tralfamadorian machines the last traceable source of control, the novel goes a long way toward implying a purely mechanical Universe. As we have observed, Rumfoord voices most of the cynicism which might be associated with such a view, but the narrative itself remains undeviating in its depiction of the human condition. Consider, for example, the account of Rumfoord's de-materialization:

> A Universe schemed in mercy would have kept man and dog together.
> The Universe inhabited by Winston Niles Rumfoord and his dog was not schemed in mercy. (p. 295)

On the other hand, there is nothing to say that the Universe is schemed in malignity. Though it frequently appears adverse, its main characteristics are shown to be its indifference and its incomprehensibility. *The Sirens of Titan* warns against performing for some big eye in the sky and looking for answers in space. It insists that believing "somebody up there likes me" is as wrong as assuming "somebody up there has it in for me," and it questions our ability to say whether there is or is not "somebody up there" at all. So the sirens come to stand for man's looking for happiness and meaning somewhere outside of himself where such things are not found. As such their siren song becomes the lure of surrender to their submarine world, of resignation to nothingness.

A criticism which has been made of William Golding is that he has devoted a succession of novels to diagnosing the shortcomings in the way man lives and the nature of his situation, but has attempted little in the direction of guidance as to how man should meet his condition. If the same criticism were applied to Vonnegut it would not be *easy* to counter. The pessimistic view of man's behavior, of his place in the Universe, implied in so much of his fiction, suggests that Vonnegut may himself feel hard put to come up with answers. Indeed, in interviews he practically confesses as much, along with admitting to the attraction of withdrawal which also appears in his work. Yet some answers are suggested, if only by reverse implication in showing what are judged as immoral, inadequate, or simply *wrong* behavior and attitudes. And *The Sirens of Titan* provides more direct answers than most of his other novels. It shows, for example, the importance of our facing the ramifications of that existential view of his condition which contemporary man has so widely accepted. It asserts that while an indifferent universe may confirm no purpose in our existence, we can give meaning to life by the way we lead it. This entails giving up the search for a rationale in the incomprehensible workings of the Universe, the hunt for some answer from above, and turning to ourselves to provide meaning. We see this change enacted in Constant, who turns from vague search for purpose to the thoughtful creation of one in a sense which approximates Samuel Johnson's in the final couplet of his *The Vanity of Human Wishes:*

With these celestial Wisdom calms the mind,
And makes the happiness she cannot find.

Finally, *The Sirens of Titan* emphasizes the need to recognize the apparently indifferent, frequently adverse Universe as the shared environment of all men, and to perceive that this makes concern, compassion, and love imperatives.

These imperatives are the reason for the warmth generated in the latter part of the novel. For Vonnegut's moral persuasions are not conveyed by hard logical argument or philosophical dialogue, but by the illustration of human consequences. They are urged less by argumentation than by the sustained force of that current of human feeling which moves through the book. It is that which provides the standard. Constant and Salo feel moved to self-negation when they both believe they have committed crimes against close friends. Both are at their best when they show love. Their roles—their being used, their courier missions, their abuses by Rumfoord, their resignations, their affirmations of love—are curiously parallel. To say this, to speak of Salo as if he were human, too, is not simply to fall for some sentimental ploy in the depiction of the robot. For the point is exactly that in becoming unreliable, emotional and compassionate, Salo does become human in the best sense. Man and robot have both refused to be reduced to machines by a mechanical Universe. This does not imply optimism or hope—the terms of the depicted Universe remain unchanged—but it does mean that the novel provides a basis of moral purpose and affirms the possibility of meaningful life. The science fiction serves not only as a source of interest, energy and fancy in *The Sirens of Titan*, but as an effective instrument of Vonnegut's moral and human concerns.

III

Mother Night: A Portrait of the Artist

Though they are strikingly different novels, *Mother Night* (1961) might be seen as extending and testing some of the premises of *The Sirens of Titan*. The later novel returns solidly to earth; it is the only one by Vonnegut which can be said to be totally shorn of the trappings of science fiction, and rather than ending with a young man grateful for life it closes with a middle-aged man surrendering it. Yet there remain strong affinities. The most obvious, brandished before us by Vonnegut in his "Introduction," is the moral "Make love while you can. It's good for you" (p. xii). Put that way, it sounds rather like "Make hay while the sun shines." Well, it is meant to: *Mother Night* might support that motto as well. But the novel does assert the value of love and the meaning of it that Malachi Constant discovers, while also going on to test whether love is enough. It also puts to a harsh test Beatrice's claim that to be used is better than to be of no use to anybody. Howard Campbell, Jr., is certainly used—by Nazis, Americans, and himself—and he loves, but in the end finds that only death can give his life meaning. Whereas in the earlier space fantasy Vonnegut uses the telescope to show us the expanse of an Absurd Universe, he now uses the microscope to show us not just the immediate context of the workings of such a cosmos, but an interior view of their operation upon one man.

Mother Night begins with an Introduction (written five years after the novel was first published) in which Vonnegut summarizes his own experience of Nazis, dwelling mostly on his being in Dresden during the intensive Allied bombing of that city. He suggests that the novel offers two morals. First, "We are what we pretend to be, so we must be careful about what we pretend to be." Second, "Make love when you can. It's good for you." The story makes clear that the second moral is not as frivolous as it might at first sound.

Then comes an "Editor's Note" which explains that what follow are the confessions of an American Nazi, Howard W. Campbell, Jr., deceased. The title, it explains, comes from a speech by Mephistopheles in Goethe's *Faust*, in which he proclaims his affinity with the universal darkness (Mother Night) which preceded the first light.

The confessions begin with Campbell in an Israeli prison not long before his death. Three levels of narrative are developed simultaneously: Campbell's early life, tracing his stay in Germany and services as Nazi propagandist and American agent during the war; his life in New York from the end of World War II up to his surrender to the Israelis; and the present of his detention in Israel. There are important interrelationships between these threads of the narrative which the immediate juxtaposing of events years apart often emphasizes. For the sake of clarity, the plot is summarized chronologically, not in the sequence in which the novel presents the action.

Born in Schenectady, Campbell moves to Germany when his father is transferred there by General Electric. He becomes a playwright of some note, and marries a German actress, Helga Noth, whose father is a city police chief. Campbell writes plays for her, and later a pornographic novel called *Memoirs of a Monogamous Casanova,* based on their imaginative sexual role-playings. As war draws near, Campbell is approached by an American who identifies himself as Major Frank Wirtanen, and asked to serve as an American agent. Partly because he cannot resist playing roles, Campbell accepts. As an American and a playwright, he fairly easily works into a position advising the Nazis on the propagandizing of America and broadcasting Jew-baiting diatribes. In public Campbell becomes known as a vicious anti-Semite, an enthusiastic Nazi and an open traitor to his native country, while in secret he is transmitting messages from Allied agents. He knows nothing of the messages himself—he even unknowingly transmits the news of Helga's death—being simply instructed to deliver his speeches with certain pauses and inflections which comprise the code. Actually, Campbell sustains this conscious schizophrenia fairly comfortably, but when he needs a refuge he finds it in "the nation of two," the private world of love he and Helga create and in which they find a separate peace from the horrors of Nazi Germany.

Late in the war Helga disappears while entertaining troops on the Russian front. Soon afterwards, Campbell takes the treasured motorcycle of his close friend Heinz Schildknecht (who, Campbell learns after the war, has also been an underground agent all along) and pays a final visit to his father-in-law and Helga's younger sister, Resi. Two minor episodes of importance occur here—the father chastizes a Russian woman slave-laborer for her careless handling of a vase, and Resi tells Campbell that she has always loved him. Many years later Campbell reads how Werner Noth died—hanged nine times (the last time fatally!) by a group of Russian and Polish women slave-laborers.

Campbell eventually surrenders to American forces who have just occupied their first extermination camp. His captor, Lieutenant Bernard B. O'Hare, forces him to look at the trappings of the camp and at six German guards strung up on their own gallows. Major Wirtanen secretly intervenes to spirit Campbell away from having to face war crimes charges, though American intelligence will not publicly acknowledge his spying mission.

Campbell takes up a life of seclusion in Greenwich Village, sustained in his solitude by the memory of Helga. By chance he begins woodcarving and accidentally cuts his thumb, forcing him into contact with some other residents in his building. One is "foxy" George Kraft, reformed alcoholic, painter, and Russian spy. The others are a Jewish physician, Dr. Epstein, and his mother. They are former inmates of Auschwitz, and while the son wishes only to forget, the mother remembers and is suspicious on hearing Campbell's name. Shortly after this, Campbell's seclusion is broken, at first only by his mail. He receives an abusive letter from his old captor, O'Hare, and copies of an American Nazi periodical, *The White Christian Minuteman*. The publisher of this racist tabloid, the Reverend Doctor Lionel Jason David Jones, had been put in touch with Campbell by foxy old Kraft, of course, and shortly afterwards pays a visit. *The Minuteman*, meantime, has betrayed Campbell's whereabouts not just to O'Hare but to the Israelis, who plan an Eichmann-style kidnapping. This threat drives Campbell into the protection of the "Iron Guard of the White Sons of the American Constitution," a pathetic fly-by-night outfit led by Jones, an old time American Nazi named August Krapptauer, and Robert Sterling Wilson, self-styled "Black Fuehrer of Harlem" and former Japanese agent.

Events now move quickly for Campbell. First, Jones' Nazis miraculously resurrect Helga, who has supposedly worked her way from Russia to East Germany to Berlin. The reunion proves shortlived—Helga turns out to be amatory little sister Resi. Then, during a meeting of the

Iron Guard, Campbell is called out by a message and meets the elusive Major Wirtanen again. This "Blue Fairy Godmother" reveals to Campbell that Kraft is a Russian spy, that Resi is, too, and that their plan to smuggle him to Mexico to escape the Israelis represents only the first step of a trip to Moscow. When Campbell returns and confronts the pair, Resi pleads that she loves him anyway, but at that point the meeting is raided. Resi commits suicide to prove her love, the others are arrested, but Campbell once more goes free under the aegis of mysterious governmental agencies.

Yet for Campbell, freedom holds only weariness and fear. He returns to his room, now sacked by righteously indignant haters of fascism, only to confront ex-Lieutenant O'Hare once more. In an upset, the former Nazi-cum-spy breaks the arm of the former hero and sends him packing. But now, with neither love nor curiosity to sustain him, Campbell gives up. He badgers the reluctant Dr. Epstein into contacting Zionist friends, and delivers himself into the hands of the Israelis.

In Israel, Campbell writes his confessions while he awaits trial. His guards interest him. Eighteen year old Arnold has never heard of Goebbels. Arpad Kovacs despises "briquets," people who did nothing to save the lives of themselves or others under the Nazis. Arpad himself played a double role of spy and viciously anti-Semite S. S. member. Among his guards, however, Andor Gutman interests Campbell most. He had become a "briquet," a volunteer for the *Sonderkommando*, the corpse-carriers who were themselves always killed. Campbell asks Gutman why he volunteered—Gutman does not know, but says the explanation would take "a very great book." That book is, of course, *Mother Night*, for Campbell has himself become a "briquet." Old Mrs. Epstein perceives this when, watching Campbell give himself up, she repeats the old Nazi call for *Sonderkommando*: *"Leichenträger zu Wache"* ("corpse-carriers to the guardhouse"). The one thing that could save Campbell from a death sentence would be some positive evidence that he was in fact an American spy during World War II. Miraculously that finally comes, for the "Blue Fairy Godmother" Frank Wirtanen now reveals himself as U. S. Army Colonel Harold J. Sparrow, breaking all his oaths to secrecy to save Campbell. But too late. Campbell finds the prospect of freedom "nauseating," and commits suicide by hanging, self-convicted of "crimes against himself."

For most of those whom it touched directly, World War II has remained the most memorable experience of their lives. This appears to be true of Vonnegut, and in particular the horrifying and puzzling experience of being under the raid on Dresden seems to haunt him. He alludes to it repeatedly in his fiction, as if compelled to somehow come to terms with it if not erase it. *Mother Night* does not deal directly with the bombing of Dresden—the raid has no part in the plot—but that, in a sense, is what the book is about. For the novel exposes and probes time and again the puzzles and paradoxes which lurk behind the horrors of war. In the "Introduction," and later in *Slaughterhouse-Five*, Vonnegut asks "Why Dresden?" How did the champions of justice and the vanquishers of tyranny come to wreak such hideous slaughter upon the hapless and militarily irrelevant city? That question invites a whole series of related queries about roles and identities and essences. Questions of who were villains and who heroes, of when heroes were villainous and villains heroic, of vice in the defense of virtue and virtue as the mask of vice, even of what was vice and what virtue. At the center of these questions stands Howard Campbell, both hero and traitor to Nazis and Americans alike. What, he must ask himself, was he? Which role was pretense, and which reality?

The questions, of course, go beyond those relating to the immediate experiences of World War II. As we see in French writers of the last three decades, the war serves as a literary testing ground for the existential philosophies it both refined and popularized. In *Mother Night*, Vonnegut uses the circumstances of the war to make graphic the existential assumptions and to intensify acutely the existential questions of *The Sirens of Titan*. Do actions have meaning in an absurd world? How can those actions be judged? How do people find purpose? Can they retain a will to live, even, and how? Why do some lose that will and go submissively to their deaths? In a world so apparently devoid of truths, with such truths as there are generally paradoxical, what hope does man have of obeying Polonius' first commandment, "to thine own self be true"? The latter is the question first in the mind of Campbell, and from which Vonnegut draws his moral for *Mother Night*: "We are what we pretend to be, so we must be careful about what we pretend to be" (p. v).

How does Campbell, knowing better, get into his position of double jeopardy? To start with, association with Nazis of greater and lesser importance came easily. The political and governmental people liked to look cultured by associating with arty people, while to Helga and Campbell the Nazi officials were simply important society people and an enthusiastic part of their audience. Campbell and Helga did not admire the Nazis, nor did they hate them, he says: "They were people. Only in retrospect can I think of them as trailing slime behind. To be frank—I can't think of them as doing that even now. I knew them too well as people, worked too hard in my time for their trust and applause" (p. 39). *Too hard,* he admits, but easily at first and perhaps naturally for a man concerned with the success of his career who regards the things going on in Germany—"Hitler and the Jews and all that"—as beyond his control and therefore none of his concern (p. 38).

In fact, Campbell's easy acquiescence, even his later trying "too hard" to please the Nazis, seems easier to understand than his accepting the dramatic but distinctly tricky proposition "Major Wirtanen" makes him. To the proposal that he become an ardent Nazi, rather than merely being polite to Nazis while working as an American agent, Campbell at first gives the logical answer: " 'No—hell, no' " (p. 40). But Wirtanen knows how to appeal to the dramatic artist. First, Campbell would become an "authentic hero" of extraordinary bravery.

Second, if he survived a war won by the Allies, he would be left with no reputation and probably nothing to live for. Wirtanen aims at what he thinks he has learned of Campbell from his plays—that he loves good and hates evil, and believes in romance. More than that, Campbell insists, it appealed to the "ham" in him, the chance to fool everyone with imaginative creation and good acting. "And I *did* fool everybody. I began to strut like Hitler's right-hand man, and nobody saw the honest me I hid so deep inside" (p. 41). The "act," the pose as Nazi, rather than the function as spy, extends the greatest attraction to Campbell. Throughout the war he never knows what messages he passes on, to whom, or from whom. All of his enthusiasm goes into the imaginative extension of his Nazi role, into fooling more of the people more of the time, while his being an agent becomes a near-forgotten incidental occasionally remembered when he needs justification.

In saying the job appeals to his "ham" side Campbell may be using what Vonnegut calls "a bit of a weasel." The confession is true but diverting. For Vonnegut and, later, Campbell himself are aware of the ambiguous role of the writer as "artist" in the way James Joyce played with it—as meaning both creator and "con-artist," the confidence trickster. The warning comes early, in the "Editor's Note": "To say that he was a writer is to say that the demands of art alone were enough to make him lie, and to lie without seeing any harm in it" (p. ix). And the note goes on to warn that playwrights are especially adept liars in manipulating lives and emotions in the artificial context of the stage. The "editor" adds the qualifications that lies told for artistic effect—"in Campbell's confessions, perhaps—can be, in a higher sense, the most beguiling forms of truth" (p. ix). Campbell cannot resist the challenge of writing for the great stage of Nazi Germany, shaping lives and passions there while remaining, like Joyce's artist, detached and indifferent as he manipulates. The catch comes in that the playwright is his own central character and actor, that it is his own life and passions that he warps, and that his theatrical deceptions become the reality in which he must live.

The writer as deceiver, trafficker in pretense, even as propagandist, becomes more than the sort of self-deriding sideline motif it frequently forms in Vonnegut's stories. From the start, from *Player Piano*, we have seen that sort of fun with writers. (In that novel we see the writer who compromises his wife rather than his artistic integrity; in *The Sirens of Titan* there are spoofs of various literary forms, including Rumfoord's "beguiling truths" in writing his own versions of history and religion.) This time there is fun, but a more serious note, too. We laugh at the disclosure that a Russian, Stepan Bodovskov, has won acclaim passing off his translations of Campbell's works as his own. Here indeed is the artist as con-man. Even Campbell appreciates the act: " 'I'm glad somebody got to live like an artist with what I once had' " (p. 151). Bodovskov, however, is shot, not for plagiarism but for originality when he, too, becomes what he has pretended to be and writes works of his own. As a sort of confidence man who deals in beguiling truths, who shapes emotions in artificial stagings and who thus tries to influence the way in which his audience looks at the world outside, the playwright—or the writer in general—is in part a natural propagandist.

Vonnegut usually plays with this conception more gently by connecting writers and public relations men. At issue is not just the financial problems the writer faces which may drive him to becoming a PR man to survive, nor simply the question of how far toward being the PR man a writer may have to compromise himself in trying to win a market by giving the audience what it wants. Vonnegut puzzles around the question of how much any writer, in working through the creation of artifice, in trying to stir emotions, or in persuading an audience to his vision of truth, might be seen as faker, public relations man, or propagandist. And he also appears to be concerned with the relationship between the "inner man" in whom the emotional need to write springs and the figure of the author who may emerge from the works, in interviews, or even as a persona in the mind of the writer himself. By having this particular writer a playwright and something of an actor, Vonnegut also makes more apparent the logical extension of these concerns about the writer—that the artist can in large measure be seen as an intensification of everyman and the relationship between what he pretends to be, his facade, and what he is, or likes to believe he is.

The double role gives Campbell freedom to indulge pretense and artifice and the extension of his public persona largely because it carries with it the assurance that he is, after all, an "authentic hero" who will in the long run only be reviled. He can thus play the role to the full with the assurance that there is, in fact, some solid substance and truth at the heart and that to do so is not merely self-aggrandizement. So we see him plunge with fervor into designing himself a Goering-like uniform for his own "Free America Corps," using Lincoln's Gettysburg Address to provide the title for a play commemorating the heroes who died putting down the Warsaw Ghetto, designing a caricature of a Jew for a shooting target, and priding himself on his skill as a "shrewd and loathsome anti-Semite."

In large part, the realization of what he has done to himself artistically, rather than the recognition of what he has helped to inflict on thousands of others, brings Campbell down. Even after his surrender, he feels disappointment when the Israeli guard who has posed as an S. S. man during the war condemns one of his old speeches as weak. " 'It has no body, no paprika, no zest! I thought you were a master of racial invective!' " (p. 23). Campbell's *Memoirs of a Monogamous Casanova,* an unpublished account of the sex-life he and Helga sustained by adopting numerous pretended roles, is another instance of his extending creative artifice and artistic persona to his real life. The diary becomes more than a record of sexual experimentation, a part of the experiment itself, making their erotic life an entirely self-conscious art. When he learns that the *Memoirs* have been published throughout Eastern Europe, *with illustrations,* he feels

97

outraged. The illustrations mutilate his words, making his record of love pornography. Hearing what has happened to the *Memoirs* jolts Campbell in the direction of awareness of what he has become: " 'The part of me that wanted to tell the truth got turned into an expert liar! The lover in me got turned into a pornographer! The artist in me got turned into ugliness such as the world has rarely seen before' " (p. 150). As it is the artist that responds to the challenge of the propagandist role, so it is the artist who first recoils from the consequences. The limitation to this reaction (which comes when he talks to Wirtanen shortly before the raid of the Iron Guard meeting) is that Campbell still blames others primarily, and feels used. When meat-packers butcher a pig, he says, they use everything but the squeal. With him they have used even the squeal.

That playing Nazi appeals to his playwright's bent should not be taken to suggest that Campbell goes through the war without qualms. Campbell admits to being aware of the madness around him as early as 1938, which is when he began to create with Helga their "nation of two." With "nothing in my life making sense but love," Campbell says, he resorted to this double bed-sized kingdom for Helga's "uncritical" love (p. 64). Outside of that private world they would behave like the "patriotic lunatics" around them, but that did not count—only their private world counted. When Helga disappears on the Russian front, Campbell is left "stateless" and unfeeling. He has deadened his emotions to all but his love for Helga—"a young lover's happy illusion" which develops into "a device to keep me from going insane"—and without her only deadness remains. So the pain and the knowledge of what he has been doing is real enough to Campbell. As he says in contrasting himself to Dr. Jones, that American Nazi was ignorant and insane, while he was neither. His instructions from the Nazis *were* ignorant and insane; he knew it; and he carried them out anyway. And later, when the Iron Guards play a recording of one of his wartime speeches, Campbell has no violent reaction, admitting, "I've always known what I did. I've always been able to live with what I did. How? Through that simple and widespread boon to modern mankind—schizophrenia" (p. 133). To sum up, Campbell does recognize his role in the horrors around him, but chooses to evade it in his worlds of artifice and pretense. Just how strong the guilt feelings were during the war, and just how difficult was the task of evasion at the time, remains rather elusive. As the "editor" warns, confessions can be lies. But this much we do know: the "nation of two" was the center of his life; the death of Helga leaves him directionless; after the war he feels his guilt; and in the confessions he feels compelled to admit that he knowingly furthered ignorance and insanity.

Campbell makes relatively few references to his being a spy in justifying his wartime activities. One suspects that he, too, knows that his Nazi enthusiasms may have exceeded what the role called for. His father-in-law, who admits to having wished he could prove Campbell a spy and see him shot, points out that it really makes little difference whether he is or not. He explains that " 'all the ideas that I hold now, that make me unashamed of anything I may have felt or done as a Nazi, came not from Hitler, not from Goebbels, not from Himmler—but from you.' " And he adds the most telling and ironic note of all. " 'You alone kept me from concluding that Germany had gone insane' " (p. 80). Even if one accepts that his enthusiasms were not excessive, but simply the skill of a distinguished spy, the moral questions remain little changed. When Wirtanen reveals that only three people knew of his spying, Campbell interprets this to mean that only three people knew him for what he was. The rest? Well, the rest also knew him for what he was, says Wirtanen, to which Campbell protests that *that* was not him. " 'Whoever it was—' said Wirtanen, 'he was one of the most vicious sons of bitches who ever lived' " (p. 138). Shocked that Wirtanen could say this, knowing of his role, Campbell asks if the Major thinks he was really a Nazi.

"Certainly you were," he said. "How else could a responsible historian classify you? Let me ask you a question—"
"Ask away," I said.

99

"If Germany had won, had conquered the world—" he stopped, cocked his head. "You must be way ahead of me. You know what the question is" (pp. 138-9).

And Campbell has to answer that he would probably have gone on much the same, as "a sort of Nazi Edgar Guest," possibly even coming to believe his own propaganda "that everything was probably all for the best" (p. 139). That sort of recognition plagues Campbell in the later years and drives him to examine his Nazism in itself. It also tends to emphasize why, during the war years, the spy role seems to remain of relatively secondary importance in his motivations; for Campbell, as for others, the pretense had supplanted the reality.

In fact, wartime Germany appears to have been less of a nightmare to Campbell than his fifteen postwar years in New York—or perhaps the greater distance of time made it seem so. Yet even when captured by Americans and made to look at the trappings of a concentration camp, his greatest interest is in the six hanged camp guards —since he expects to be hanged himself—and the peace they seem to have found. Campbell finds no such peace, making his way to Greenwich Village to take up an existence of tortured solitude or, as he calls it, "purgatory." New York becomes a purgatory mainly because he knows there are those who would still like to capture him. As he watches the children playing hide-and-seek, he longs to be able to echo their call of "Olly-olly-ox-in-free" (p. 30), and end the too-real game in which he himself is caught. That wish itself echoes Wirtanen's warning in 1938 that when it was all over, nobody would call him out of hiding with "Olly-olly-ox-in-free" (p. 45). Alone in his "ratty attic," without that concentration of his emotions on Helga which had been the axis of his mental stability during the war, he becomes a "death worshipper." For thirteen years he lives on four dollars a day (though worth about two hundred thousand), talking to the ghost of Helga. It is indeed a purgatory, a prolonged suspension between condemnation and execution, life and death. And it is a purgatory of his own making.

Purgatory begins to look more hellish—or perhaps more properly purgatorial—once Campbell begins to stir to life and make contact with the outside world. This happens when he becomes childishly enthused over wood-carving—his first artistic endeavor since the war and per-haps a sign that some purgation has indeed taken place. Woodcarving leads him to meet foxy old Kraft, the blun-dering Russian spy, who in turn makes sure others know of Campbell's existence. With the exception of Dr. Epstein, those he comes into contact with—Kraft, the assorted American Nazis, O'Hare—resemble a motley collection of rejected aspirants to a rogues' gallery. But they facili-tate the bringing of Campbell to a final accounting with himself. Burlesque parodies of Allied "right" and Nazi "evil," they force Campbell to confront what he has been. On the one hand there are the anonymous veteran who kicks him senseless with one blow for each dead GI buddy, and O'Hare who believes he has a divine mission to destroy Campbell as the personification of pure evil. On the other hand are the enfeebled Iron Guard, chant-ing their cardiac-arrested way up the stairs to offer friend-ship and protection to the champion of racial purity. Finally comes Helga-Resi so that his old axis, too, is renewed and tested.

When "Helga" reappears "as blithe and blooming" as on her wedding night, save only for snow-white hair, we suspect something even though we want it to be true. Campbell wants it to be true so much that he suspects nothing. The "nation of two" reestablished, his manu-scripts returned, Campbell again turns from the surround-ing world. The revelation that Helga in fact is Resi sets him back, though he has not known the difference and has sworn their love could survive anything. As he looks at a great Victorian double bed in a shop window he sees superimposed on it their reflections in the glass, like two ghosts, one of an old man, the other of a girl young enough to be his daughter. He does not recognize the "allegory" he suspects the scene portrays, but we may surmise it has something to do with living in the past, on a ghost of what has been, on a dream whose unreality

101

has become ludicrous. Resi has pretended to be someone else, Campbell in loving her has thought himself back in the past and identified himself with what he is no longer. As he again becomes involved in a dangerous situation, with threats to his life, Nazis and spies around him, he resorts to the same course he had followed before. Or tries to. Because this time, in the absurd parody of his former state, nothing holds up and much is reversed.

First Campbell forgives Resi's deception and accepts her as Helga again, although she increasingly asserts her own personality. Together they plan a new "nation of two"—perhaps of three, since Kraft is to be included—in a life of love, writing, and escape in Mexico. Campbell at this point, with unwitting irony, praises the miracle of Resi's "power to raise the dead" (p. 126). The irony, of course, is that Resi has not just revitalized Campbell, but has brought back to life the old one of the war. To escape the Israelis and assorted other moral avengers, Campbell take shelter with Dr. Jones' Nazis. Soon he is in the midst of a meeting, listening to a recording of one of his wartime speeches; seeing again his caricature-Jew shooting target; evasively playing along with these bizarre misfits whom he privately refers to as "Hottentots." But Resi does wean him of Helga, while the Nazis are such a ludicrous reenactment of the Third Reich and his American pursuers such distortions of patriotism and defense of right, that the whole experience—part nightmare, part Laurel and Hardy—helps trigger his awareness of what he has been, has become—*is*.

With Wirtanen's intercession to warn that Resi and Kraft are Soviet agents bent on spiriting him to Moscow, Campbell's world again collapses. Kraft, as the spy the Russians wish to eliminate, who therefore might want to really escape, and who genuinely is smitten with the playwright as artist, is the one man Campbell could trust, Wirtanen says. But Campbell, ironically echoing what Wirtanen had earlier said of him, will not trust a spy. Resi, whom the Russians plan to threaten to force compliance from Campbell, pleads that she, too, really intended to escape with him, but again Campbell cannot trust a spy. His lack of response to Resi's pleas, however, goes deeper than that. Having used love as an escape, having loved the phantom of Helga, having even been willing to go on accepting Resi as Helga, Campbell is now offered the devotion of a woman prepared to love on any terms, even to die for him, and finds himself unable to meet it. He cannot even give her any reason for wanting to go on being alive. By this time he has no such wish himself.

Again released by the grace of his "Blue Fairy Godmother," Campbell "freezes." He is immobilized not by guilt, which he has taught himself not to feel; not by a sense of loss, since he covets nothing; not by rage at injustice, for he no longer expects fairness; not by being unloved, having taught himself to do without love; not by death, which he sees as a friend; not by the thought of a cruel God, because he expects nothing of Him—but by "the fact that I had absolutely no reason to move in any direction" (p. 167). Eventually prodded toward home, he recalls as he mounts the stairs the times he had climbed to his bomb-shattered Berlin apartment with Helga. Arriving at the top of those splintered stairs with her, to gaze into open sky, he had "felt like Noah and his wife on Mount Ararat."

> And then the air-raid sirens blew again, and we realized that we were ordinary people, without dove or covenant, and that the flood, far from being over, had scarcely begun. (p. 173)

With no "dove or covenant," no one to cry "Olly-olly-ox-in-free," no end to the nightmare and the threats, no fear even of the ultimate threat of death, no purpose in living, and now not even any curiosity to see more of life, Campbell turns himself in to the Israelis. His surrender becomes grotesquely appropriate. Like some Anne Frank, he has spent years hiding in a ratty attic. Like those Jews to whose pogrom he had lent verbal support, he has his door smashed down and suffers visitations from "patriots" who, as Mrs. Epstein notes, resemble those who came in the wake of the S. S. even to their taking the lightbulbs from the stairway. Like the Jews, he has been told he is to be taken somewhere for relocation when he was really being shipped to his death. When the "three heroes" come to collect Campbell in the middle of the night, they bang loudly on the front door like so many S. S. Finally, his going with them has its sinister parallel, which old Mrs. Epstein recognizes in saying that he *has* to go. *"Leichen- träger zu Wache,"* she croons—"Corpse-carriers to the guardhouse" (p. 187). The propriety of his end rests not simply in the fact that he suffers the same fate he has helped to inflict upon others, but that he has reduced him- self to the same state, has committed the same crime against himself as against the Jews.

Campbell, then, has told the story of how he, like the *Sonderkommando* his guard Gutman was to describe, came to hand himself over to certain death. Gutman, who had himself volunteered for the job but had been spared it, cannot explain his action and is ashamed of it. All he can say is that after two years of hearing music over the speakers, music invariably broken into by that crooning call for the corpse-carriers, it " 'suddenly sounded like a very good job' " (p. 21). Campbell says that he can understand that. Perhaps we can, too, in that we have seen how the "music" in his life—the nation of two, play- writing, Resi—has always been interrupted. And always there has been the succession of fears and losses and deaths, and no covenant, no dove. He has become, appro- priately, a man like Macbeth, "supped too full of horrors."

Yet while he, like Macbeth, claims to be left devoid of feeling, he *does* feel. Without it he would be incapable of the degree of self-recognition he achieves in his Israeli prison and of his final self-condemnation and execution. We also, of course, have the word of another guard, Mengel. Mengel says that during the war he became so that he could feel nothing, that most of the men he knew then and the war criminals he had seen since were the same way, but that Campbell has a bad conscience, ap- parent from his troubled sleep. We may be left unsure how much guilt Campbell actually feels. Certainly he never

104

waxes emotional with regret for those murdered by the Nazis. He seems to judge that the widespread crimes against humanity perpetrated during the war are largely in the nature of the way of the world. When his young Israeli guard, Arnold Marx, tells him about Assyrian Tiglath-pileser the Third, who burned down Hazor after Solomon rebuilt it following an earlier Assyrian sacking, Campbell feels the ancient dust of the Holy Land creeping over him. That refrain from *The Sirens of Titan*— "everything that ever has been always will be, and everything that ever will be always has been"—seems to become part of his awareness. At the time he gives himself up to Epstein he observes: "His mother understood my illness immediately, that it was my world rather than myself that was diseased" (p. 185). There is also the letter he says he would write to "Creative Playthings, Inc.," about education. He would educate children not to expect peace and order, but to be eaten alive; to learn that people are greedy and why, how they lie, and what makes them go crazy (pp. 190-191). And at the last he bids a farewell so preposterously hackneyed as to stress simultaneously its irony (since he has been responsible for so much cruelty in the world) and its poignancy: "Good-bye, cruel world!" (p. 192).

Campbell obviously experiences something close to existential nausea. He has seen so many people dazed and robbed of feeling—children who sit unblinking listening to the bombs "walking" over the shelter, the child Resi who dispassionately hands over her pet dog to be killed, concentration camp inmates who walk willingly to death, Mengel who feels no more strapping the ankles of a man about to be hanged than in strapping his suitcase—that he has been brought to the same senseless state himself. He has come to it out of the belief that he can somehow retain an unscathed inner self while acquiescing to the horrors around him. That course, which contributed to the dehumanizing of others, led to the dehumanizing of himself. It is that crime against himself for which he condemns Howard Campbell to execution.

Campbell's self-execution retains its ambiguities, however. It might be argued that his death sentence is motivated less by rational judgment of himself than by his nausea of "dreadful freedom" in the existential sense or, less philosophically, by the knowledge that freedom would only continue the interminable game of hide-and-seek. But both of those conditions are implicit in his recognition of his crime against himself. It might be argued that in terms of the moral Vonnegut supplies the story, Campbell remains a fraud, and that his "real self" is the Nazi and his role as the spy the pretense. Part of that assertion, obviously, has truth. But it is precisely the recognition of the degree to which he has become what he pretended to be which Campbell regards as the crime against himself. He recognizes that in identifying his "real self" with the spy role he has condemned it to equal secrecy; that his admission that had the Nazis won he would have gone on as "a Nazi Edgar Guest" would then have meant the simultaneous annihilation of spy role and inner self. And it might also be argued that the confessions are "beguiling truths," a self-justification, and that Campbell remains in reality no more repentant or contrite than some other Nazi war criminals. In so far as his confessions can be trusted at all, Campbell confronts that issue. In contrasting himself to Adolf Eichmann and his naïve defense that he had only been following orders, Campbell argues that he has always had a discriminating mind: "I always know when I tell a lie, am capable of imagining the cruel consequences of anybody's believing my lies, know cruelty is wrong" (p. 124). Later he differentiates himself from those "nations of lunatics" like Dr. Jones possessed of "the classic totalitarian mind, a mind which might be likened unto a system of gears whose teeth have been filed off at random" (p. 162). He, says Campbell, has never willfully destroyed a tooth on the gears of his mind. Such self-recrimination might be viewed as lies directed toward a more imaginative self-defense than Eichmann's, but they are harsh recriminations to leave in one's final record. Is Campbell, then, primarily concerned in his confessions to reestablish to the world the existence of that "inner self" which no one any longer believes in? If so, the lies can indeed

106

become truths, for if Campbell *does* lie from concern for his "inner self" we know that core remains. Ultimately, although ambiguities and realistic complexities persist, although good and evil are shown to be not always what they seem, the book is certainly not without a moral frame. Campbell's self-judgment and execution take place within that moral frame, and their essential implications are apparent.

The moral impact of *Mother Night* is sustained by more than logic and exempla, however, and its complexity far exceeds the morals Vonnegut offers at the opening. The characterizations are successful to the point that one becomes involved with Campbell and others, and drawn into the moral issues that confront them. Campbell may remain frequently difficult to sympathize with, and he is not always a character with whom one can feel empathy, yet somehow, by the end of the novel one is caught up. We find ourselves hoping that an escape to Mexico may prove possible, or that Major Wirtanen will after all materialize with the saving letter, even though at the very moment we may feel uncertain that is what we should want. Similarly, while we may halfway expect the reverse that comes at the end—that the letter will come but that Campbell will die anyway—we are not untouched by his decision to die, even knowing that life might be worse for him or feeling that his death is deserved. We come to care about Campbell even though his generally detached, frequently wry, rarely self-pitying narrative voice does not directly ask that we do and in spite of our knowledge of his crimes.

The other important characters similarly emphasize the moral purpose of *Mother Night*. Some explicitly reinforce the warning that one becomes what he pretends to be. Resi does this by, in effect, becoming the Helga she has pretended to be. Unfortunately, Resi's characterization does not quite come up to the role assigned it. Even at her dramatic and pitiable death it is easy for us to hold something back. We have not known her well enough or long enough. She remains part stunned little girl, part ghost of Helga, and we are not sure where the loving younger sister leaves off and Soviet spy begins—perhaps because this is how Campbell himself feels about her. Resi has been too much the chameleon for us to be unreservedly moved even by her final pleadings and declarations. Other characters work well, however, even when they are not developed much beyond caricatures. Vonnegut is generally good at exploiting stereotypes for the swift delineation of lesser characters, or, conversely, at breathing life into stereotypes. The American Nazi Dr. Jones makes a good example in this category, and Kraft, the spy who stayed out from the cold, another. For both of these old rogues we feel something more than what comes with the release in tension at discovering they are not the fiends we first expect; something, in fact, remarkably close to affection. That, too, serves the moral ends of the novel.

Characteristically, Vonnegut has no outright "bad guys" or villains, and in a book with the cast of *Mother Night* that must be considered remarkable. Adolf Hitler almost appears—he sends a note saying he was moved close to tears by Lincoln's Gettysburg Address. For the wrong reasons, of course; but the response is so nearly right and the note such a joke that even the Fuehrer seems beguilingly harmless. Eichmann and Goebbels, too, are shown with their pants down, as it were, rather than as demi-devils. Werner Noth treats a slave woman badly and obviously worries more about his vase than the condition of the woman, but he is basically an honest cop and hardly deserves his horrifying death. O'Hare somehow registers as the most menacing and vicious character, but his hatred is so pathological, his psychological state so understandable and his threat finally so empty that he, too, fails as a villain. As Campbell tells O'Hare, there is " 'no good reason ever to hate without reservation. . .' " (p. 181). That, too, is a moral the story exemplifies.

What of the other moral in Vonnegut's "Introduction": "Make love when you can. It's good for you"? It has been preceded by another: "When you're dead you're dead." This latter provides the context for the whimsical tone of the love moral. But beyond that, one senses that Vonnegut wants to assert the value—the imperative, even—of love

108

in a world such as *Mother Night* describes, but shies away from any solemn statement of it that might sound trite or sentimental. Love is on test, however, in *Mother Night*. It forms the axis of Campbell's life in 1938, and he plans to write a play on the theme, entitled "Nation of Two." "It was going to show how a pair of lovers in a world gone mad could survive by being loyal only to a nation composed of themselves—a nation of two" (p. 37). Ultimately, that kind of love proves inadequate. The "nation of two" provides a safe haven, mutual support and a source of beauty in their lives, but it also has elements of evasion, illusion and egocentrism. Because of it Campbell can dissociate himself from the horrors around him and put from his mind his own part in them. He lauds Helga, who does not know of his role as spy, for her "uncritical love" of him as he plays Nazi:

> No young person on earth is so excellent in all respects as to need no uncritical love. Good Lord—as youngsters play their parts in political tragedies with casts of billions, uncritical love is the only real treasure they can look for (p. 44).

The truth of that statement is undeniable. Yet there remains a flaw in the way Campbell applies it. Campbell's love is too egocentric—almost an "I know I've been a bad boy, Mommy, but don't you chide me, too" attitude. And more than that, he sets artificial boundaries on love. His *Memoirs of a Monogamous Casanova* becomes an entirely appropriate record, for he is monogamous to the point that his only extension of love is in erotic role-playing. The phantoms of their private world become more substantial to him than the real people around him.

Erotic, romantic or uncritical love can help sustain but remains inadequate, especially if it becomes an escape from the responsibilities a more universal love would demand. Simply, Campbell's private love becomes an alternative to brotherly love of his fellow men. In a real sense he *uses* love to sustain not just his "real self" but also the public "pretended" role. It seems ruthlessly fitting that his love of Helga is *used* by spies, that it should be reduced to a kind of necromania during his New York purgatory, and that he should be led to feel he has betrayed it with the spy sister who pretends to be his real wife. That cruel working of Nemesis in part explains why he cannot tell Resi that "love is the only thing to live for" (p. 160). Certainly private love is not. Shortly after Resi's death, Campbell says, "I had taught myself to live without love" (p. 167). While he speaks here of withstanding being unloved, which might indicate he has come to dispense with uncritical love, there are other implications. Campbell *exists*, rather than lives, without love. Resi's arrival as Helga does, as he says, reawaken his artistic energies while the illusion lasts. In one way the statement is true: he had taught himself to live without real love of his fellow men. In another sense, it is false: as Resi detects, Campbell's tragedy is that he is so used up that he cannot love any more or that he refuses to act on that love. Nor in the last analysis can he live without love. With Resi dead and the ghost of Helga laid, he becomes immobile. And his failures in love are not the least of the crimes committed against himself which he condemns.

Eros alone proves insufficient sustenance, the novel suggests, but it can help and certainly has its powers. It provides the most beautiful and memorable moments in Campbell's life. Resi's dying for love cannot lightly be dismissed; in a perhaps backhanded way, it stands as one of the most affirmative, positively human actions in the book. Even Jones has two happy marriages (and happy marriages are not that common in Vonnegut), the first of which actually makes him forget his racial obsessions. But the obvious appeal of *Mother Night* is to "Make love when you can" in a more general sense—something perhaps approximating the hackneyed "Make love not war." That kind of love *is* good for you. Seen in this way, prefaced by "When you're dead you're dead," Vonnegut's moral comes out not too different from W. H. Auden's imperative: "We must love one another or die."

Apart from *Slaughterhouse-Five*, *Mother Night* shows more human misery in "realistic" situations than any of

110

Vonnegut's novels, yet it is far from solemn. Typically, Vonnegut's sense of the absurd brings out the ludicrous, the preposterous, the simply slapstick in even the darkest situations. He achieves that precarious balance, which contributes so much to the effectiveness of his best work, between awakening us to the dangers he sees and dissolving the terrors of our world in laughter. A fine example of this function of the humor comes in the depiction of Eichmann. Jokingly, Campbell asks him if his defense will be that he was only a soldier taking orders from superiors like any other soldier. Eichmann is astonished that Campbell knows the contents of his secret defense statement. The warning within the laughter is quickly underlined: "This man actually believed that he had invented his own trite defense, though a whole nation of ninety some-odd million had made the same defense before him" (p. 123). Similarly, the nauseating horror of Werner Noth's multiple hanging is at once countered and heightened by the equally nauseating but ludicrous way it has been presented on the magazine's cover. The asexual old hags have become girls with "breasts like cantaloupes, hips like horse collars, and their rags were the pathetic remains of night-gowns by Schiaparelli" (pp. 85-6). Generally, the more grotesque the horror, the more easily it seems to lend itself to comic preposterousness. In *Mother Night,* Vonnegut reminds us effectively that the nausea-evoking existential concept of the Absurd is, after all, a comic one. That does not make the terrors any less, but it does provide us with another way to look at them. And seeing the funny side of things usually helps.

Mother Night contains some of the most amusing satire in Vonnegut, too. Much of it focuses on various brands of "patriotism"—the last refuge of the screwballs and political cranks depicted. The American Nazis—Dr. Jones, Krapptauer, Father Keeley and the Black Fuehrer—are the subjects of the most ridicule, but their German proto-types fare little better. The satire of Jones works particularly well because it is developed at some length and in detail. His final lecture to the FBI agent about saving the country from international Jewry and the Communists might look rather trite by itself, but it succeeds in context because it has been well prepared for. In the course of satirizing Jones, Vonnegut does an excellent job of debunking Bible colleges giving mail order diplomas, the absurd minds of racial bigots, racist publications, gun clubs, Ku Klux Klan, and even the U. S. Government charges on which Jones was imprisoned during the war. Some of the joke-barbs are *almost* old stuff, but seem so typical that they fall into that "we know it could be true" category. For instance, there is Krapptauer's thesis that "the Pope was a Jew and that the Jews held a fifteen-million-dollar mortgage on the Vatican" (p. 63). Or Dr. Jones' book proving that Jesus Christ was not a Jew because none of the fifty assembled portraits reveals Jewish jaws or teeth. Campbell, on the other hand, has the most perfectly Aryan set of teeth Jones has seen, short of Hitler himself. Names once again contribute to the satire. The always "foxy" Kraft is not crafty enough. To him goes the distinction of having the only Soviet spy ring staffed entirely by American agents. Father Keeley, defrocked, alcoholic and bigoted, has done anything but go straight. The phonetics of Krapptauer (crap-tower) also have possibilities. Added to these are such spoofs as the Black Fuehrer's conviction that Japanese are "colored" but Chinese are not, or the "Iron Guard" leader who must stop and count at every third stair to save his heart from failing, so that every kind of comic material is thrown into the satire.

Another kind of humor—perhaps *sly* best describes it—creeps into this novel to undercut at almost every turn. It enters from the start with the suggestion that Campbell's confession that his life has been a lie, may itself be full of lies. After all, Campbell's saying in his confession that "I always know when I tell a lie" gives no assurance he is telling the whole truth now. We have seen him try to "put on" Eichmann, and sense that that is part of his style. This comes out in his own comment on his broadcasting—a comment which may also be a little less than the truth although it contains some obvious truths: "I had hoped, as a broadcaster, to be merely ludicrous, but this is a hard world to be ludicrous in, with so many

112

human beings so reluctant to laugh, so incapable of thought, so eager to believe and snarl and hate" (p. 120). But to turn to some specific undercuttings. Several of them seem especially designed to poke at Campbell's central claim that the racist broadcaster was not the *real* Campbell. For example, the one thing which convinces him that the amazingly well-preserved woman before him *is* Helga is her *white* hair. Or there is his stockpile of Crosby recordings of "White Christmas." Both evoke echoes of Jones' newspaper, *The White Christian Minuteman*. And his final wish, that as he hangs he will not hear "White Christmas," seems all too appropriate to a man accused of being a white racist. References like these cause us to wonder, if only fleetingly and half-seriously, if they are not some kind of Freudian slip. That half-pause is enough to do the job.

Different in nature but similar in effect, in arousing an at least passing suspicion, are Wirtanen's statement that he could never trust Campbell because he was too good a spy and Noth's distrust of him as a Nazi. Our distrust of Resi and of Kraft helps undercut our willingness to believe Campbell who, like them, has also pretended to be other than what he protests he is. Then, too, there are the testimonial letters Kraft and Jones give to the Israelis. Jones says simply that Campbell is "a saint and a martyr in the holy Nazi cause" (p. 189). Kraft opines that Campbell was an ardent Nazi but a political idiot and "an artist who could not distinguish between reality and dreams" (p. 189). In effect, Campbell does become a martyr to the Nazi cause. And a major reason for his ever having accepted his role, and for his continuing, has been that as an artist he confused reality and dreams. Those truths make us think for a moment and about the rest of the testimonials. Though both statements reflect the personal obsessions of their crazy writers, and appear at first invalid, Campbell's later indictment of himself gives some credence to their essence. Characteristically, Vonnegut enjoys keeping us a little off balance, unable to say finally that "this is so," just as he refuses to remove from his

113

fiction the uncertainties, the qualifications, the unknowns which persist in our vision of daily reality.

The fact that the comedy works so well in a story full of human anguish, rarely becoming strident in its biting irony and preserving its poise in the satire, is one of the qualities which distinguish *Mother Night*, certainly in comparison with *Player Piano*. Another respect in which this novel compares well with the previous two is in its greater unity. To begin with, it has more unity of time and place. There are three main time periods and three places, but they telescope neatly into one another. It is also less episodic, the flashbacks and time-shifts operating within the three-tier time structure, giving little sense of fragmentation, or wandering. The framing of the story with an "Editor's Note" and "Introduction" also provides focus, as do the morals Vonnegut posits there. By and large, the novel holds that focus, keeping as its principle subjects betrayal of self, war (as a manifestation of the absurd), and love. Finally, the steady development of the central character through first-person narration adds to the unity and direction. Many of the qualities which contribute to the merit of *Mother Night* are the very ones which also make it perhaps Vonnegut's most traditional novel in form. Paradoxically, perhaps, that also accounts for the relative weaknesses of the book. For *Mother Night* lacks some of the excitement and verve of *The Sirens of Titan*, for example, and it is sometimes less likely to carry its reader along than that earlier, more wandering fantasy.

There remain two lines of continuity from the earlier novels which deserve mention. The note of nostalgia, so strong in *Player Piano*, and the temptation toward evasion, toward opting out, both reappear. Nostalgia works powerfully on Proteus and Campbell because both find the present distasteful. It might be argued, however, that Proteus' nostalgia exists earlier and in large part prompts his dissatisfaction with the present, whereas Campbell's nostalgia grows with his anxiety about the present. While Campbell's nostalgia does not equal Proteus', it has almost equally important results. One could say it helps shape his destiny, since his writing of historical romances might

indicate a deep-rooted yearning after simpler, more romantic times, and that this is the element in his artistic
temperament which responds to playing the Nazi role. The
same bent emerges in his "sultan and slave girl" games
with Helga, contributing to their insulating love. He looks
longingly at the children playing hide-and-seek, wishing
then and at other times that he could cry "Olly-olly-ox-
in-free." In New York he lives on memories of Helga,
and his nostalgia for the "nation of two" blinds him to the
improbability of Resi's pose. And, finally, what could
be more nostalgic than this?

I'm dreaming of a White Christmas,
Just like the ones we used to know.

Obviously, much of this nostalgia becomes a form of
evasion and reflects the wish to opt out of intolerable
situations. The repeated desire to hear a voice call, "Olly-
olly-ox-in-free" certainly does. So, too, does his wish for
some covenant, some dove, to signal that the deluge has
ended and life can begin anew. The "nation of two," of
course, becomes another attempted escape, a narcotic
which lets his "emotions be stirred by only one thing—
my love for Helga" (p. 47). Campbell's dazed state that
leads to his surrender to the Israelis shows a strong desire
to withdraw from a world he thinks diseased, and from
responsibility. Mrs. Epstein describes him as not the first
man she has seen "who longed for someone to tell him
what to do next, who would do anything anyone told him
to do next" (p. 185). Finally, his suicide, although charac-
terized as self-execution, might be seen as the ultimate
opting-out, as suggested by his laconic farewell: "Good-
bye, cruel world!" (p. 192).

Opting-out, or withdrawal, comes in for rather stern
judgment in *Mother Night*, even though in the circumstances of this novel any temptation toward it becomes
understandable. The conditions in Nazi Germany gave
evasion an undeniable appeal, and in addition Campbell's
dual role, catching him as it were between a rock and a
hard place, makes the attraction of that cozy private

world of uncritical love readily comprehensible. But finally not excusable. Campbell makes that point himself when he condemns Eichmann's "trite defense" that he was only a soldier obeying orders as the same evasion offered by "ninety some-odd million" Germans before him (p. 123). Being a spy and intending to be merely ludicrous as a broadcaster are other evasions possible to Campbell, but he comes to recognize that they do not excuse his actions. Yet what *Mother Night* indicts most vigorously is the withdrawal from responsibility to oneself and to others. At the most superficial level, the example here is Campbell's belief that he can feign the evil role and remain the pure soul. The obvious warning is that to withdraw in the midst of a society one feels morally superior to means sharing moral responsibility for the continuance of what one disapproves. And that to act disinterestedly means to become uninvolved—virtually a condoner of the things one would claim to reject—with all the crime against self that implies. Campbell's final "Auf wiedersehen?"— "Until we meet again"—points directly at the reader and the fact that we are all, to a greater or lesser degree, likely to have shared this crime with him.

The other principal area in which withdrawal fails concerns love. That love between two people is a fine thing needs no belaboring—although Vonnegut does portray an atypical number of successful romances in the novel to emphasize the point. But to narrow love to the exclusion of compassion for one's fellow men contradicts the very essence of love. It then becomes egocentric, and therefore not love at all. Not to love one's fellow men, *Mother Night* would show, means to acquiesce in their suffering. And that is to warp one's own being, to surrender in effect if not intent, to "hate without reservation," or finally, to dehumanize oneself.

Mother Night, then, stands as a morally determinate work for all the ambiguities and undercutting. The ambivalence which, in particular, surrounds the truth of Campbell's confessions and the motives behind his suicide-execution, reflects Vonnegut's hesitation to sermonize, his intent to capture the complexities of life, and his compassion for men fated to live in an Absurd Universe. Here Vonnegut takes some of the practitioners of perhaps the greatest crime of our time and, while not for a moment condoning their actions, considers them with humanitarian understanding. That is why the range of emotions, the personal interaction, the intensity of feeling—be it of hate, love, fear, or simply amusement—is greater in this book than in most of Vonnegut's, and needs to be. To balance the undeviating indifference of its universe, *The Sirens of Titan* needs the assertion of love and the tone of warmth with which it ends. Those elements support the moral affirmation of that novel—even if they are undercut. In *Mother Night,* with its equally arbitrary world, the warmth of human feeling is necessary to counterbalance the frightening manifestations of existential nothingness and to emphasize the moral direction taken.

What finally of the undercutting in the book? Of the lingering uncertainties as to whether Campbell's death represents an act of self-judgment or simply escape from a cruel world? Campbell is an artist writing a final portrait of himself. He is apparently aware of those Joycean ambiguities concerning "artist" and "forger," having lived by deception and knowing all about lies. He is also a writer with a feel for the ludicrous, and a declared hope to make his audience laugh and think (p. 120). There may be as much reason to suspect that he might *wish* to tantalize his readers with the thought that he was a Nazi now duping us with a repentant confession, as to suspect that such is genuinely the case. The fact that this writer of almost offhand tone, who claims to be left with no feeling, so repeatedly searches his emotions, would tend to support this view. Moreover, the very uncertainties they contain lend credence to the authenticity of the confessions as a man's struggle to know himself.

Our final recourse, however, in measuring not just the honesty of Campbell but the moral stance of the novel itself, should be to *Mother Night* as a portrait of Vonnegut as the artist, too. Behind the mask of Campbell is the mask of Vonnegut. He also likes to keep the reader guessing, enjoys the ludicrous, wants to evoke laughter

117

and thought, and adopts a seemingly offhand tone. He, too, not just in creating Campbell but repeatedly in other works, shows an almost obsessional awareness of the artist as forger, confidence trickster, PR man, deceiver. All of that accounts for much of Vonnegut's ironic undercutting, and it also points to his concern to be honest. In *Mother Night* he confronts quite directly man's condition in an absurd world, using terms closely related to the wartime experience which, more than any other, made manifest that condition to him. To say that the undercutting demolishes the truth of Campbell's assertions or any moral affirmations in the novel would be to say that Vonnegut had, in fact, surrendered to the meaninglessness of the universe. It would mean that finally he saw nothing beyond the ludicrousness itself, that he believed that nothing really made any difference, that he was, in effect, a nihilist. And that he clearly is not. Page after page of the novel shows Vonnegut as a man who feels affection, hurt, indignation, compassion, injustice, and sorrow. Awareness of the absurd is there; meaninglessness is faced unflinchingly; but Vonnegut does not submit to the darkness of nothingness as Mephistopheles does in the quotation from which the book draws its title. He recognizes that we are each a part of that original darkness, but affirms "that supercilious light" in its struggles against "Mother Night." That is the portrait of the artist *Mother Night* finally gives us. That is the source of the human warmth in the novel which irresistibly supports its moral thesis.

IV

Cat's Cradle:
"No Damn Cat, No Damn Cradle"

If one had to select the novel which best examplifies the methods and techniques of Kurt Vonnegut, there would be plenty of good reasons for choosing *Cat's Cradle* (1963). No doubt some readers would argue that what Vonnegut actually does in this novel is to parody himself. There are plenty of good reasons for supporting that position, too. What one can safely say at the outset, however, is that *Cat's Cradle* illustrates almost every device, technique, attitude and subject we encounter in Vonnegut, and is filled with particulars which echo other novels. At the same time, compared with the two preceding novels, it seems thinner in plot, more superficial and fragmentary in characterization, weaker in its ability to evoke emotion or concern, and consequently less substantial. That is at least partially explained by the nature of the book. Call it an anti-novel, surrealistic, fantasy, one big "put on," or whatever: the one thing it should not be called is a representational novel. For in *Cat's Cradle,* the paradoxes of artist and deceiver, truth and lie, reality and pretense, as propounded in *Mother Night,* are projected into a sustained game.

Cat's Cradle is narrated by a free-lance writer named John, but who begins by saying "Call me Jonah"—an echo which sets the tone for the novel—so Jonah he will be. Jonah has been working on a book to be called *The Day the World Ended,* the story of August 6, 1945, the day an atomic bomb was dropped on Hiroshima. As material for this work, Jonah wants to find out what went on in the household of the late Dr. Felix Hoenikker, one of the fathers of the bomb, on that date. Accordingly, he writes to Newton ("Newt") Hoenikker, one of the three children of the scientist. Newt writes long letters in reply which reveal that the father had little interest in the bomb on that day, nor in his children on any day.

A year later, Jonah travels through Ilium where Dr. Hoenikker had worked, and pokes around to see what he can pick up for his book. Among other things, he discovers that Hoenikker's other son, Frank, had been a scientifically minded child who was gifted at model making but so socially inept and secretive that the other children had called him "Secret Agent X-9." He had left town during his father's funeral, never to be seen again, although stories had him involved with a group of gangsters running stolen cars from Florida to Cuba on war-surplus LSTs. The daughter of the family, Angela, had acted as mother to both brothers and her father. Unattractive and over six feet tall, she had never dated, but had suddenly married a handsome man named Conners.

Jonah also visits the research establishment where Dr. Hoenikker had worked. There he learns that Hoenikker had been involved with a project to enable the Marines to get out of mud. His idea had been to invent a new basis of crystallization for ice, so that water would freeze at higher temperatures. This variant becomes "*ice-nine*," although it is spoken of only hypothetically, nobody at this point believing it possible. The nightmare quality of *ice-nine* which haunts Jonah is that once used, it would start a chain reaction which would turn all of the world's water to ice.

Soon afterwards, Jonah sees a newspaper supplement on the Caribbean island of San Lorenzo. Two things strike him about this: first, the photograph of Mona Aamons Monzano, a "heartbreakingly" beautiful blonde mulatto who is the adopted daughter of the island's president; second, the revelation that the republic's "Minister of Science and Progress" is none other than the long vanished Frank Hoenikker.

Assigned to do a magazine story on San Lorenzo, Jonah sets out on an airliner in which he encounters several other people, all bound for the island, who assume significance in the story. There is Horlick Minton, a diplomat discredited during the McCarthy witch hunts and now assigned to end his days as Ambassador to San Lorenzo. With him is his wife Claire, and the two are obviously engrossed in each other to the point that they largely discount the rest of the world. A second couple is Hazel and H. Lowe Crosby, crass God-fearing Midwesterners on their way to set up a bicycle factory on the good non-unionized, anti-communist island. At San Juan, Newt Hoenikker and Angela join the flight, bound, Jonah discovers to his despair, for the wedding of Frank and the haunting Mona.

On arrival in Bolivar, capital of San Lorenzo, the Americans are welcomed by President "Papa" Monzano, whose characterization appears to owe something to Haiti's late "Papa Doc" Duvalier. "Papa" collapses, abbreviating the ceremony but giving Jonah time to observe Mona engaged in a curious game of footsie with a fighter pilot. That footplay, he soon discovers, is one of the rituals of the outlawed religion of "Bokononism."

Bokonon is a black from Tobago whose given name was Lionel Boyd Johnson. In a series of bizarre travellings, which include taking courses at the London School of

Economics and meeting Ghandi, he joins up with a Marine deserter named Earl McCabe. The two are ultimately washed up naked on the shores of San Lorenzo, become its governors, and set about making it a Caribbean Utopia. All economic programs fail, so they decide to give the people circuses. Bokonon becomes a religious leader, McCabe the political head of state. By mutual agreement, Bokonon and his religion are outlawed, both to give the religion some zest and to occupy the people in searches for Bokonon. The idea is to provide the island life with some "Dynamic Tension" through the opposition of fugitive good in the country and controlling evil in the city. A huge hook is erected, from which are to be hanged Bokonon and any of his followers. "Papa" Monzano, in succeeding McCabe, has perpetuated the game, although he—like everybody else on the island—is in secret a Bokononist.

Other important people on San Lorenzo are Julian Castle, a one-time dilettante become resident Albert Schweitzer, operating his House of Hope and Mercy in the jungle; Dr. Schlichter von Koenigswald, a former Auschwitz physician making atonement in Castle's service; and Castle's son Philip, who paints, writes, and owns the hotel.

When "Papa" collapses during the arrival ceremonies he names Frank as his successor. Frank quickly calls Jonah to his house and persuades our narrator to become president in his place, partly by pointing out that whoever accepts the post will marry the divine Mona. They arrange that the announcement of Jonah's succession will be made the next day following a ceremony commemorating the Hundred Martyrs of Democracy—a hundred San Lorenzan volunteers drafted immediately after Pearl Harbor to join American forces. This San Lorenzan contribution to the war ended a few minutes after it began, when their ship was torpedoed just outside the harbor.

In the interim, however, "Papa" ends his sufferings from cancer by swallowing the contents of a small vial he keeps around his neck. To the amazement of Dr. von Koenigswald, the corpse at once turns hard as iron. As

122

soon as the doctor puts his hands in water, the doctor turns hard as iron, too. Jonah realizes that Felix Hoenikker *had* discovered *ice-nine,* and that Frank had some of it which he had used to buy his position with "Papa." Later, Jonah learns that Angela had bought her "tomcat husband" with *ice-nine* which then found its way into the hands of the U.S. Government, and that Newt's brief affair with a Ukrainian midget from the Bolshoi ballet company had put *ice-nine* in Soviet possession, too.

Next day's commemorative ceremonies involve an air display by San Lorenzo's six piston-engined fighters. In the course of their attacks on targets representing Mao, Stalin, Hitler, Kaiser Bill and others, one catches fire and crashes into the cliff face below the castle. The castle crumbles, part of it sliding into the sea, bearing with it Ambassador Minton and wife who ride down hand in hand, smiling contentedly. The castle's collapse also sends the "frozen" body of "Papa" into the sea, and in a moment all water turns to ice, the land becomes frosted, and the skies fill with funnel clouds. Mona and Jonah escape into a bomb shelter oubliette, where they remain for seven days. When they emerge, they discover that the Crosbys and Newt are still alive, too. They also discover a hollow where numerous Bokononists have committed suicide together by touching *ice-nine* frost to their lips. To Jonah's chagrin, Mona does likewise.

The remaining survivors live for several months, Newt painting, Hazel sewing an American flag, Crosby cooking and Jonah writing his book. To the best of their knowledge, they are the only people on earth. As Newt and Jonah drive into town for supplies, Jonah relates how he would like to climb the island's highest mountain to plant some symbol more meaningful than "Mom" Crosby's American flag, but he does not know what that symbol could be. At that moment he sees Bokonon sitting beside the road. Jonah goes back and asks Bokonon what he is writing. On the paper which he hands Jonah, Bokonon has written that if he were a younger man he would write "a history of human stupidity," climb the mountain, swallow *ice-nine,* "and I would make a statue of myself, lying

123

on my back, grinning horribly, and thumbing my nose at You Know Who" (p. 191). We are left to assume that the book is the one we have read, which would also, of course, satisfy Jonah's original intention of writing *The Day the World Ended*.

Not so long ago, a group of thirty thousand or sixty-five thousand (depending on one's point of view) persons marched from Minneapolis to St. Paul to honor those slain at Kent State University and to protest the United States' invasion of Cambodia. When they arrived in St. Paul, they were harangued by a black speaker who noted the absence of black marchers and the failure of the demonstrators to be equally active in behalf of minority groups. "So as far as I am concerned," he concluded, "this whole thing is a farce! A farce!" And those foot-weary pilgrims hailed him with a chorus of "Right on!" Now to some in that audience this response smacked of paradox. How could anyone march nine miles, frequently with obvious manifestations of distress, and yet regard it as a farce? But many there *did* see the whole demonstration as an enormous "put on," while still feeling that it was worth every step of the way. To them, in fact, it was only worth the effort if it were a put on, especially if it could be a really grand one. The very fact of murders at Kent State and of "incursions" into Cambodia was evidence enough for them that to suppose more marches would actually alter the course of events was ludicrous. Understanding that is a little bit like understanding *Cat's Cradle*.

"Call me Jonah." With that beginning, so overtly echoing the most famous line in American fiction—the opening of Melville's *Moby Dick*—Vonnegut sets the tone for the novel. (It is also characteristic that Vonnegut's speaker should be a Jonah, who does in effect get swallowed by the whale, rather than a whale-hunting Ishmael.) He signals clearly the spoofing nature of the work and the fact that what we are dealing with is wholly fiction. Melville's opening seeks to evoke verisimilitude by introducing us to a narrator who seems real and who recounts a story which could be true as if it had actually happened. By contrast, Vonnegut immediately invokes a famous novel and an improbable Old Testament story (as well as a name associated with ill-luck) as if to insist that the narrator is purely a fictional persona and his story all make-believe. Rather like one of those plays where the actors pause to talk with the audience about the roles they are playing, *Cat's Cradle* glories in its own artifice. Traditional "serious" novels tend to work on the premise that the illusion of objectivity and of verisimilitude is essential to the psychological manipulation of the audience. *Cat's Cradle* comes as close as it can to warning us that objectivity and verisimilitude in fiction are illusions, and it makes little pretense of being other than illusory. That aspect of the novel is also underlined by an extension of the ambiguities about the writer as liar which arise in *Mother Night*. Jonah quickly announces himself a Bokononist, while the views of Bokononism form a steady perspective throughout the novel. And the first sentence of the *Books of Bokonon* reads: " 'All of the true things I am about to tell you are shameless lies' " (p. 14).

In *Cat's Cradle* there are, in a sense, three writers at work. There is Vonnegut the author, and within the world he creates, Jonah, and within the story he narrates, Bokonon writing his *Books*. All three seem aware that, as the "Editor's Note" to *Mother Night* says, "lies told for the sake of artistic effect . . . can be, in a higher sense, the most beguiling forms of truth." And *vice versa*. Each of these three writers is concerned with truth, using the word repeatedly, and appears to feel great need to declare the truth of the human condition. Yet each also warns of the writer's willingness to lie in behalf of his truths, and cautions that the truths that he sees may themselves be lies. (By now, of course, we are indeed in a world where it takes all the running you can do to stay in the same place—intentionally so.) In this respect, the kinship between writers and religious preachers which Vonnegut has pointed toward before becomes explicit. The fusion is complete in Bokonon. As a religious leader, Bokonon grows out of Lasher of *Player Piano* and Rumfoord of

125

The Sirens of Titan by way of the propagandist Campbell of *Mother Night*. Lasher, through his Ghost Shirt Society, provides a myth and a hope for people who need them, without believing in either. Rumfoord manipulates his Martian invasion to bring the peoples of Earth together and returns Space Wanderer Unk to confirm his Church of God the Utterly Indifferent. Through these two staged "lies" he teaches his "truth" that "I was a victim of a series of accidents. As are we all." What Campbell intends as ludicrous lies become the sustaining truths by which live such men as Noth, Krapptauer and Jones— and so many more. To a varying degree, each of the preachers lies about the nature of the world in order to give it a semblance of coherence. Each contrives to make circumstances appear to be reducible to truths. That in part is what the writer does in shaping his fiction. And that is what Bokonon unashamedly admits to doing—while warning that all he says is lies. As Jonah says, "Anyone unable to understand how a useful religion can be founded on lies will not understand this book either" (p. 14). Bokononism, then, might be the box within the box within the box we start with.

Ostensibly, Bokononism is born out of the failure of McCabe and Bokonon (Johnson) to make tangible improvements in the life of San Lorenzo. It becomes a way of looking at life which is predicated on the notion that things are rough all over and that it is unrealistic to expect that man can make them much better. Bokononism partly parodies "Rumfoordism" in its assumption that things do not just happen, they are *meant* to happen. Bokononists always say "as it was meant to happen," instead of "as it happened." Bokonon develops this concept when so many coincidences shape his travels that he decides something is trying to get him somewhere for some purpose. In Bokononist terms, however, it translates roughly as saying there is no decipherable meaning in the workings of the world, but that we can play as if there were some. Or, "there are more things wrought in Heaven and Earth, Horatio, than are dreamt of in your philosophy." Another Bokononist expression of this is "Busy, busy, busy," which

126

we are told, "is what we Bokononists whisper whenever we think of how complicated and unpredictable the machinery of life really is'" (p. 51).

Much of Bokononism, then, builds around the notion that there are incomprehensible forces determining our lives. Or that there are not, but that it is generally helpful to proceed as if there were. These characteristics of the religion become apparent in an examination of some of its terms. *Zah-mah-ki-bo*, in its most reducible simplicity, means fate or inevitable destiny. *Zah-mah-ki-bo* is why Jonah must assume the presidency when Frank has not the stomach for it—or so Frank says. Then there is the *karass,* a team of people organized "to do God's Will without ever discovering what they are doing" (p. 11). People whose lives become inexplicably involved with one's own might well be in one's *karass*. If this does not take care of enough coincidences, there are the *vin-dit*, the *wampeter* and the *wrang-wrang*. The *vin-dit* is a personal experience which pushes one in the direction of Bokononism, a coincidence which in other religions might be called a revelation. A *wrang-wrang* works the other way, being "a person who steers people away from a line of speculation by reducing that line, with the example of the *wrang-wrang's* own life, to an absurdity" (p. 59). A *wampeter* is an object, idea, or event around which the lives of a *karass* rotate. *Ice-nine*, for example, becomes the *wampeter* of Jonah's *karass*. Just about nothing that can happen to a man in this busy, busy, busy world lacks a place and explanation in the mysteries of Bokononism.

In social affairs, too, Bokononism proves a useful religion. It observes, for example, that a *karass* of only two people, called a *duprass*, cannot be invaded even by the couple's own children. A *duprass* is a version of what in *Mother Night* is called a "nation of two," the example of it in *Cat's Cradle* being Mr. and Mrs. Minton. Despite being so totally engrossed in each other, the Mintons come off looking fairly good. At least they go to destruction hand-in-hand while the rest of the world looks on, rather than the other way around. And they do not appear to have used their *duprass* as an evasion of all concern for others. Nations of more than two do not fare as well. They fall into the category of the *granfalloon*. A false *karass,* "a seeming team that was meaningless in terms of the ways God gets things done," a *granfalloon* might be illustrated by "the Communist party, the Daughters of the American Revolution, the General Electric Company, the International Order of Odd Fellows—and any nation, anytime, anywhere" (p. 67).

The cardinal sin to a Bokononist is to be a *sin-wat*: " 'A man who wants all of somebody's love' " (p. 141). Mona accuses Jonah of being a *sin-wat* when he wants her to give up playing footsie with all and sundry. The notion that his prospective wife can love everyone as much as him distresses Jonah. The notion of monogamous pedal relations distresses Mona. For this footplay, in which the two participants press the soles of their bare feet together and knead, is *Boko-maru,* the Bokononist ritual for the meeting of souls. *Boko-marual* promiscuity seems to be what keeps San Lorenzo running. This tactile game points toward the one serious element in Bokononism. Late in the story Jonah asks Frank Hoenikker if nothing is sacred to Bokononists.

"Just one thing."
I made some guesses. "The ocean? The sun?"
"Man," said Frank. "That's all. Just man." (p. 143)

Everything else in Bokononism might be *foma* (lies), but the sanctity of man rings true. It is, after all, the central concern which leads Bokonon to formulate his religion of *foma.* And that same concern for man remains the one constant at the center of the deceptions and dichotomies and verbal diversions of *Cat's Cradle.*

The sanctity of man provides the foundation for Bokononism's essentially satirical view of the world. It is the reason why Bokononism so frequently and adeptly pinpoints human folly. For the follies exposed, be they individual or institutional, usually qualify because they falsify man or his condition. Religions, especially Bokononism itself, fit into this category. As Julian Castle explains in relating the birth of Bokononism, " 'Truth was the enemy of the people, because the truth was so terrible, so Bokonon made it his business to provide the people with better and better lies' " (p. 118). The representative of Christianity on the island, Dr. Vox Humana, with a doctorate from the Western Hemisphere University of the Bible of Little Rock, Arkansas—contacted through a classified ad in *Popular Mechanics*—understands the same religious principle. He embellishes his ceremonies with bell, butcher knife and live chicken, fulfilling (though presumably not for the chicken) the motto of his *alma mater*: "MAKE RELIGION LIVE! "(p. 145). Science, too, is a pack of *foma* to the Bokononist. One ironic episode involving science occurs as "Papa" is dying. "Papa" tells Frank to *really* kill Bokonon, and to teach the people truth through science. " 'Science is magic that *works*' " (p. 147). Immediately thereafter, he asks for the Bokononist last rites. (Science really does work for "Papa," of course: he commits suicide by *ice-nine* and takes the rest of the world with him.) By and large, however, Bokonon's attitude toward religion, science, and most other systems is summed up in one of his characteristic poems:

Tiger got to hunt,
Bird got to fly,
Man got to sit and wonder, "Why, why, why?"
Tiger got to sleep,
Bird got to land,
Man got to tell himself he understand (p. 124).

That, as he sees it, is the function of science, and politics, and religions, including his own. And he makes his answers to the "Why, why, why?" particularly beguiling by telling us that they really are not answers at all. At the same time, both the poem and Castle's remark about the people's need for better lies indicates a compassion for man even in folly.

If Bokononism derides itself and insists on exposing its own role as the happy hoodwinker, it also says that this is just what a good religion should do, and it leaves us concluding that in spite of its *foma* it tells a few home

129

truths about a number of subjects. Literature is approached in much the same way in *Cat's Cradle*. As a matter of fact, we are even given testimonials by physicians which support both arts in similar terms. Julian Castle praises Bokononism because it works, adding, "I couldn't possibly run that hospital of mine if it weren't for aspirin and *Boko-maru*'" (p. 177). That thorough scientist, Dr. von Koenigswald, says he agrees with only one Bokononist idea: " 'I agree that all religions, including Bokononism, are nothing but lies!'" But he adds, before he gives "Papa" Bokononist last rites, " 'I will do anything to make a human being feel better, even if it's unscientific'" (p. 148). The judgment on literature comes when Jonah discusses the possible consequences of a universal writers' strike. Philip Castle suggests people would die " 'like mad dogs, . . . snarling and snapping at each other and biting their own tails.'" Old Julian Castle concludes that without literature, people would probably die of " 'putrescence of the heart or atrophy of the nervous system.'" And he pleads, " 'For the love of God, *both* of you, *please* keep writing'" (p. 156). "Mom" Crosby adds the confirming view of the man in the street to the solemn judgment of the physician. She likes "a good laugh," and sees Jonah's last days as well spent since he is writing " 'books that make us laugh'" (p. 185). Behind the sardonic view of religion and literature lurks a premise implied in the Bokononist definition of maturity as " 'a bitter disappointment for which no remedy exists, unless laughter can be said to remedy anything'" (p. 134).

In short, Bokononism sets out to enable man to tell himself he understands, while really not explaining anything. All its explanations, it confesses, are lies, and it disclaims having any remedies. Unless, that is, offering something people can pretend to believe in is a remedy, or unless Bokononism itself can be laughed at and the laughter proves a remedy. The implied analogy with literature would be that it, too, is an expression of and a response to man's need to tell himself he understands; that it cannot really provide any answers or remedies either, unless perhaps it can evoke laughter with remedial power. Those may not be the terms in which every reader would wish to view either religion or literature, but they are the ones the narrator points to when he says, "Anyone unable to understand how a useful religion can be founded on lies will not understand this book either" (p. 14). And they are terms which go a long way toward explaining Vonnegut's method in *Cat's Cradle*. Neither Vonnegut nor Jonah asserts outright that his story is all lies, as Bokonon does, but each repeatedly shows a similar awareness of his literature as artifice and warns his audience that it is, much as Bokonon does with his religion. That stance does not imply a complete abdication of moral purpose or concern. Just as Bokononism has its roots in Johnson's despair of alleviating the sufferings of the San Lorenzans, Jonah and Vonnegut start from similar emotions—perhaps specifically triggered by Hiroshima and Dresden. In any event, both the religion and the novel undercut themselves, revel in their artifice, and offer laughter—if that can remedy anything.

Perhaps the most striking indicator of the overt delight in artifice in this novel emerges in the diction. The accents and the Bokononist terms leave their mark on the reader, who in turning from *Cat's Cradle* to the daily newspaper may catch himself railing about the *wrang-wrangs* who govern this *granfalloon*. Vonnegut revels in the very artificiality of words. A fine example comes when the German doctor administers Bokononist last rites to the dying San Lorenzan president:

> "*Gott mate mutt,*" crooned Dr. von Koenigswald.
> "*Dyot meet mat,*" echoed "Papa" Monzano.
> "God made mud," was what they'd said, each in his own dialect. (p. 149)

Here Vonnegut plays with the fact that the words do not just sound different, but in a sense become different in the three accents, just as he does in offering the transcription of "Twinkle, twinkle, little star" in San Lorenzan:

> *Tsvent-kiul, tsvent-kiul, lett-pool store,*
> *Ko jy tsvantoor bat voo yore . . .* (p. 78)

131

Our reaction might resemble that of a schoolboy on his first day in a German course listening to the Lord's Prayer in a language that is double-Dutch to him yet recognizing the Prayer. The same *thing* is so different when put into other symbols, but somehow it *is* the same. Words are toyed with as symbols in *Cat's Cradle,* and as symbols, therefore, artifice. The Bokononist terms, for example, so often sound right—*Zah-mah-ki-bo* for inevitable destiny, or easier ones like *wrang-wrang* or *sin-wat.* Or they may do the reverse—like *karass* (unless it derives from "class" or "caress")—and surprise us as nonsense symbols which emphasize the playful nature of the game. Bokonon's pun on "soul" and "soles" delights, as puns do, in the ludicrous juxtaposition of starkly different objects with phonetically similar symbols. Even "Lowie" Crosby's obsession with the word "pissant" shows a fascination with language and, more importantly, the way in which language can actually shape the formulation of ideas. Words themselves, then, are artifice. Bokonon might even say they were lies. Inasmuch as we so often substitute the symbol for the object or fail to see beyond the word itself, they might be lies. An example of this occurs when the Ilium bartender asks, " 'Didn't I read in the paper the other day where they'd found out what [the basic secret of life] was?' " Then it dawns on him. " 'Protein,' the bartender declared. 'They found out something about protein' " (p. 28).

At other levels, too, Vonnegut calls attention to the fiction, the non-reality of literature. As noted, the "Call me Jonah" opening smacks of declared artifice, and perhaps the ending, with its hints of the old tale-without-an-end technique, does the same. Another example of Vonnegut's openly bursting literary balloons comes in his description of female breasts. In *Player Piano,* a prostitute has "bosoms like balloon spinnakers before the wind." In *Mother Night,* the women in the magazine depiction of Noth's hanging have "breasts like cantaloupes." There are throw-away similes, debunking themselves in their Pavlovian verbal response. But now comes Mona, and the idea is made explicit. "Her breasts were

132

like pomegranates or what you will, but like nothing so much as a young woman's breasts" (p. 138). Vonnegut invariably plays with names and does so again in this novel, once more underlining the unreality of the work. Dr. Vox Humana is the most obvious example. "Little Newt" Hoenikker seems aptly named, perhaps with some play on "minute." Franklin and Newton, both named for scientists, are sons of the father of the atomic bomb, each in his way as monstrous as their nuclear sibling. Angela is anything but that in her physical attributes, but she does make heavenly music.

Possibly the most open display of uncloaked artifice, however, appears in the echoes of other novels. Vonnegut may be playing to his following in this, rather like a comedian reminding his audience of past jokes, or he may be consolidating a repertoire of characteristic episodes, or he may be parodying himself. Whichever the case, the effect becomes the same—the undercutting of any pretense that the fiction is more than that. For example, Johnson/ Bokonon develops his "conviction that something was trying to get him somewhere for some reason" while working at the Rumfoord Estate in Newport. Tralfamadorians, perhaps? Jonah's reaction to the picture of Mona reminds us of Constant's first look at the 3-D photograph of the sirens on Titan. Then there is the *duprass,* with its obvious kinship to the "nation of two," while in a more generalized way *granfalloonery* resembles *Mother Night's* commentaries on patriotism. Another echo of that novel is in Hazel Crosby's giving her American flag six-pointed stars of David, just as Howard Campbell had done in designing the crest of his Free America Corps. There is also the fact of McCabe and Bokonon becoming what they pretend to be, " 'McCabe knowing the agony of the tyrant and Bokonon knowing the agony of the saint' " (p. 120). Similarly, Frank's finding human beings such an inconvenience to science (p. 187) sounds a lot like Ed Finnerty's complaint that " 'if it weren't for the goddamn people . . . earth would be an engineer's paradise.' " There are, too, lesser but conspicuous echoes, like the returns to Ilium and Indianapolis. Related to these reiterations in their effect are other devices which announce the non-representational nature of the novel. San Lorenzo, for example, where Frank has become Minister of Science and Progress, looks rectangular from the air and altogether like the model country the boy Frank had built on a square of plywood. And that monstrous phallic tombstone over Emily Hoenikker's grave is obviously there more to spoof literary Freudianism, or as a surrealistic image, than for verisimilitude.

As well as laughing self-consciously at its own artifice, the novel resembles Bokononism in its satirizing other "remedies" of human suffering and purposelessness. The major targets are similar, at the head of the list being science. The main weakness of science, the satires would indicate, is that the public stands excessively in awe of it as "truth," while the scientist tends to become so absorbed in its explanations of the parts that he forgets the whole. "Papa" calls science "magic that *works*," and the average man seems to be no less superstitious. To the Crosbys, anyone against science must be a "pissant"—why, without penicillin Hazel's mother would not still be alive at a hundred and six, and Hazel herself would be dead. Even "Lowie" would not be alive but for sulfathiazole (pp. 157-8). Dr. Breed, research director under whom Felix Hoenikker worked, pleads the case of "pure" science on other grounds: " 'New knowledge is the most valuable commodity on earth. The more truth we have to work with, the richer we become' " (p. 36). It is Breed who, having acted as a sort of foster grandfather to the atomic bomb, tells the simple secretary Sandra that the world's troubles stem from people's being superstitious rather than scientific, and advocates the study of science as the cure. Others take a different view. Another secretary, Miss Faust, has her doubts about science, even if it does lead to truth. She says, " 'I just have trouble understanding how truth, all by itself, could be enough for a person' " (p. 44). Breed's son is also disaffected, and on the day of Hiroshima quits the Research Laboratory saying that " 'anything a scientist worked on was sure to wind up as a weapon, one way or another' " (p. 27).

The view of scientists in *Cat's Cradle* is quite close to that which Dr. Breed accuses Jonah of trying to make him admit to: " 'that scientists are heartless, conscienceless, narrow boobies, indifferent to the fate of the rest of the human race. . .' " (p. 35). Not that this would necessarily make them so different from the rest of the human race, seems to be an implication. But at least *the* scientist of the novel, Dr. Felix Hoenikker, does quite well at meeting Breed's specification. On the day the first atomic bomb was tested, another scientist turned to Dr. Hoenikker after the explosion and said, " 'Science has now known sin!' " To which Hoenikker responds, " 'What is sin?' " (p. 21). In both passages, and consistently in the characterization of Hoenikker, there is an element of double satire, Vonnegut making fun of the usual way of making fun of the scientist. That, too, is characteristic of the tone of *Cat's Cradle*. But that particular criticism of the scientist, his propensity to stand outside of human affairs, remains one that is repeated in the novel. Hoenikker's son, Frank, becomes the subject of it several times. One instance occurs when he refuses the presidency, preferring to play Dr. Strangelove to someone else's president. Another comes when he takes control of cleaning up the room after the deaths of Monzano and von Koenigswald— caused, of course, by his "*ice-nine*." "I could see him dissociating himself from the causes of the mess; identifying himself, with growing pride and energy, with the purifiers, the worldsavers, the cleaners-up" (p. 162). The application of this to the scientist is readily apparent. A similar point is made from the opposite tack by von Koenigswald when he defends his use of Bokononism by saying he will use anything, even the unscientific, to alleviate human suffering. He adds, " 'No scientist worthy of the name could say such a thing' " (p. 148). The criticism is summed up by Jonah when he realizes why Frank wishes him to be president. Frank wants to be freed "to do what he wanted to do more than anything else, to do what his father had done: to receive honors and creature comforts while escaping human responsibilities. He was accomplishing this by going down a spiritual oubliette" (p. 151).

What the novel would appear to conclude is that scientific knowledge cannot provide the answers to essentially human problems, but that people all too often think it can; that science is frequently exploited to create human problems, while scientists do too little to prevent this; and that the scientist may put his incomprehensible truths before other people, but turn away from the human truths life may present him. The metaphor for all of this is Hoenikker's thrusting his "cat's cradle" under the nose of Newt, who can see only a handful of string—"no damn cat, no damn cradle."

The Bokononist story of the creation records how God breathed life into mud and made man, who then sat up and asked, " 'What is the *purpose* of all this?' "

"Everything must have a purpose?" asked God.
"Certainly," said man.
"Then I leave it to you to think of one for all this," said God. (p. 177)

In that endeavor, man has been assisted by science and religion. Religion, the novel suggests, has proved rather more helpful, having greater flexibility for suggesting purposes and at the same time the means for making man feel better about his lack of purpose. Religion does not have to be cramped by the scientist's concern with truth, either. In fact, Bokonon's success hinges on his ability to supply "better and better lies" to counter the painfully obvious, terrible truth that "was the enemy of the people" (p. 118). As he puts it in one of his calypsos:

I wanted all things
To seem to make some sense,
So we all could be happy, yes,
Instead of tense.
And I made up lies
So that they all fit nice,
And I made this sad world
A par-a-dise (p. 90).

Bokononism, one might argue, makes a rather far-fetched

136

joke of religion. Yet, if one needs a touch of realism, the closeness of Bokononism in purpose and Dr. Vox Humana's brand of Christianity in form to, for example, Haitian Voodooism, should provide it. In sum, the satires of religion point compassionately to the search for purpose and the sufferings which demand it, half comdemn and half understand its tendency to hide the pains it either cannot or does not remedy, and question its propensity to make answers out of things we cannot know. That is how Newt once again has the last word. " 'Religion!' " he says. " 'See the cat?' . . . 'See the cradle?' " (p. 124).

Assorted other "remedies" come in for their share of mocking in *Cat's Cradle*. Sex, as is frequently the case in Vonnegut, proves unsatisfactory—*Boko-maru* works better. When Jonah at last gets his long yearned for Mona into bed the result is disastrous, leaving him gnashing his teeth and confessing, "Suffice it to say that I was both repulsive and repulsed" (p. 178). Later, Jonah and Newt commiserate each other on their lack of sexual urge, or even of dreams, and conclude that the hopelessness of their situation, making reproduction futile, has unmanned them. Burning lust does not last long in Vonnegut's wasteland. Various forms of *granfalloonery*—nationalism, Hazel's "Hoosier pride, capitalism, East versus West—are debunked as well. One attack in this quarter, on patriotism and war, generates particular interest because it seems more sober than most. That is Ambassador Minton's speech commemorating the "The Hundred Martyrs of Democracy"—themselves such a cruel farce. In an address which points to *Slaughterhouse-Five*, Minton refuses to consider the Martyrs as men who laid down their lives for their country, but mourns them as children murdered in war. Of the words on the wreath's inscription, "PRO PATRIA," he asks, " 'What do they mean, anyway?' "

"They mean, 'For one's country.' " And then he threw away another line.
"Any country at all," he murmured (pp. 170-1).

Medicine, perhaps the most obvious of remedies, seems

not to be mocked in itself, but is treated rather ironically and shown to be up against hopeless odds. Ironically, of the two practitioners in the novel, Julian Castle comes to medicine after years of extravagant debauchery, and von Koenigswald to atone for service at Auschwitz. Castle explains von Koenigswald's situation: " 'Yes. If he keeps going at his present rate, working night and day, the number of people he's saved will equal the number of people he let die—in the year 3010' " (p. 127). The message in that, of course, has implications for more than physicians alone.

Remedies of the spirit as well as of the body are subject to some derision. Several of the arts, including writing, become targets. Bokonon, for example, insists on the value of historical records, observing ironically that without them people of the future cannot be expected to avoid the errors of the past. Jonah, obviously, and Vonnegut by strong implication, share Bokonon's opinion that this often-expressed notion is indeed a laughable one—to any reader of historical records. Literature, as we have seen, is often aligned with religion, especially religion of the Bokononist kind. When Philip Castle mistakes him for a drug salesman, Jonah corrects him: " 'I'm not a drug salesman. I'm a writer.' " " 'What makes you think a writer isn't a drug salesman?' " asks Castle (p. 106). Of all the arts, music seems to fare best. Nobody expects Angela's clarinet playing to be anything but bad, yet when the intoxicated, six-foot-plus, horse-faced woman plays, her music is movingly beautiful. Mona's xylophone playing, likewise surrounded by irony in that her subject is invariably the painfully appropriate "When Day is Done," also proves excellent. Newt is the painter of the group. At Frank's house he works on an almost completely black canvas which evokes the interest of Julian Castle:

"It's *black*. What is it—hell?"
"It means whatever it means," said Newt.
"Then it's hell," snarled Castle.
"I was told a moment ago that it was a cat's cradle," I said.
"Inside information always helps," said Castle (p. 115).

The exchange makes some amusing commentary on both the artist's and the beholder's problems with abstract art. Castle's final judgment, incidentally, is that it " 'is a picture of the meaninglessness of it all! I couldn't agree more' " (p. 116). And with that he throws it into the waterfall. Actually, his judgment is not far off. As an "illustration" of a cat's cradle, Newt says it reflects the way in which children look at all those X's of string and see " '*No damn cat, no damn cradle*' " (p. 114).

All incomprehensible X's. No cat. No cradle. That sums up man's dilemma as the novel shows it. With no remedies—unless laughter can be said to remedy anything. And *Cat's Cradle* supplies plenty of laughter. Much of it works directly to attempt a remedy by emphasizing the ludicrous in the painful, even the tragic. After all, the way the world ends in *Cat's Cradle* is comic in form and in the far-fetched circumstances which bring it about. Even the nature of Jonah's death—if we assume he follows Bokonon's suggestions—becomes ludicrous. What could be touchingly sad repeatedly dissolves in comic incongruity. For example, there are the children at the death of Emily Hoenikker, left to their own devices and trying to find some adequate symbol for their emotions, choosing that enormous phallus inscribed "MOTHER." Or there is the well-known episode of Dr. Hoenikker leaving his wife a tip after a good breakfast. Much of the random humor has its painful element, as when Jonah says to the undertaker " 'It's a small world,' " to which the response comes, " 'When you put it in a cemetery, it is' " (p. 50). We see this dark humor again when Crosby describes to Jonah how "the hook" works. It is thrust through the offender's belly, " ' and there he hangs, by God, one damn sorry law breaker.' 'Good God!' 'I don't say it's *good*' said Crosby . . ." (p. 69). A great deal of this humor of the incongruous relates to what was said earlier about the form of the novel, too. The tip and the phallus, for example, are perfectly good symbols in their own ways, but each seems outrageous in the given context. The same principle applies when the Christian priest, Dr. Humana, uses a chicken, knife and bell in his rituals. The bell Jonah can understand as a symbol long used in Christianity, but the chicken and the knife? Surely they are associated with Voodooism or some pagan rite? Hazel's six-pointed stars, in the same way, are ludicrous on an American flag, although completely appropriate on at least one other. So that again we come back to those X's of string which should symbolize a "cat's cradle" but are not convincing.

How well does laughter then function as a remedy? The answer to that may be personal and subjective, but laughter is a remedy that has stood the test of time well. Court jesters have undergone changes, but vie with other providers of remedies in claims for the antiquity of their profession. Humor of the kind shown in *Cat's Cradle* seeks to make the injustices, pains and incongruities of life more bearable by emphasizing the ludicrous aspects of their make-up. An awareness of the Absurd can bring existential nausea, but it can bring laughter, too. One of Camus' illustrations of the Absurd in *The Myth of Sisyphus,* for example, speaks of a single man armed only with a sabre charging a machine-gun nest. Harsh comedy, but comedy nevertheless. In *Cat's Cradle* the laughter often hurts at least a little. It is also often derived from a pessimistic long-run view which renders immediate folly dismissable. Yet there is plenty in the novel which remains genuinely funny, and some rather ghastly things are reduced to jokes.

That leaves the question of how pessimistic *Cat's Cradle* is, finally, and whether its humor might not really be an expression of the bleakest cynicism or, ultimately, nihilism. Without much doubt cynicism abounds. Bokononism, of course, is founded on cynicism. Nihilism is another matter. Even to the cynical Bokononism, man is sacred. For that we have more than the word of Frank, for even in Bokonon's suggesting that his followers kill themselves with *ice-nine* and in his final note—both cynical beyond question—compassion for the plight of men is strongly implied. If Bokonon goes a little mad in his role, as Julian Castle suggests, it is at least partially explained by his frustrating inability to do anything more concrete to

140

remedy the human condition. Like most cynics, he can be seen as a frustrated idealist; and the same judgment might be ventured of Vonnegut.

The Fourteenth Book of Bokonon has a long title: " 'What Can a Thoughtful Man Hope for Mankind on Earth, Given the Experience of the Past Million Years?' " Its content consists of one word: " 'Nothing' " (p. 164). Julian Castle, as noted above, looks at Newt's painting and acknowledges that if it is a portrayal of "the nothingness of it all" he agrees. And for Newt, everything comes down to X's which are meant to signify something but do not. In using that image of the cat's cradle—or of no cat, no cradle—for the title and the central symbol of the book, Vonnegut implies an endorsement of Newt's assessment. All of this might be seen as making *Cat's Cradle* more than pessimistic (which it clearly is), but nihilistic, too. There are reasons to argue against that judgment, however. At the very time when Jonah feels most inclined toward nihilism, toward being overwhelmed by "the meaninglessness of all," he encounters his *wrang-wrang,* Krebbs. Krebbs *is* a nihilist, and his "nihilistic debauch" of Jonah's apartment, which includes a Red Guard-like hanging of the cat (and the numerous references in the novels suggest Vonnegut has a good feeling for cats), turns Jonah away from that philosophy (p. 59). Admittedly, the incident is treated comically, virtually as slapstick, but it makes a point. Partly it demonstrates that nihilism fails because of its lack of love or compassion or consideration. And even in the fantasy world of *Cat's Cradle*, those qualities remain virtues. They may be imperfectly realized, and they may come in for their share of derision, but they continue to exist to a degree which lifts the novel above nihilism.

Love hardly receives the ringing endorsement accorded it in the two preceding novels. In *Cat's Cradle*, where everything is turned upside-down, reverse implications often count. Such is the case with the strongest declaration on the subject of love. That comes when good Miss Faust affirms that " 'God really *is* love. . .' " (p. 44). The statement is in trouble from the moment of its utterance. The irony of its being spoken by a Miss *Faust* begins the novel's characteristic undercutting. Following that come the numerous questionings of the existence and nature of God, of man's pretensions to know anything about God, and certainly of God's equation with love. On the other hand, Miss Faust's assumption gives her some stability in a world which surrounds her with the incomprehensible, and her simple faith looks quite good in context. Felix Hoenikker can only ask, " 'What is God? What is love?" (p. 44). Not knowing love seems a worse crime in him than not knowing God. Perhaps what we are shown, then, is the simple girl who sees more human truth than the scientist, and whose affirmation of love may therefore be of value. Another of Bokonon's poems might be relevant at this point:

A lover's a liar
To himself he lies.
The truthful are loveless,
Like oysters their eyes! (p. 157)

Miss Faust may be deceiving herself, but the consequences of that are not as bad as the "loveless" state of the "truthful" Felix Hoenikker, whose incapability of human feeling or love toward wife, children and fellow man brings disaster at every level.

Refusals of love are invariably hurtful and bring damaging results. All three children suffer psychologically from their father's indifference, and all three end up buying love or a place of belonging with *ice-nine*. That, of course, has much to do with the final disaster. One could almost say that the world ends because a father could not show his children love. The denial of love is touched upon in another context, too. Minton has been condemned at his loyalty hearings for a sentence his wife wrote: " ' "Americans . . . are forever searching for love in forms it never takes, in places it can never be" ' " (p. 71). The Ambassador argues the point further, in relation to American foreign policy, by saying that it is regarded as treasonous to say that Americans are not loved wherever they go. It would be more realistic, he says, to recognize hate than to imagine love, and to accept the fact that all kinds of people are hated in all kinds of places. This argument gains support in the novel, first in that Americans are shown to be as capable of hating people by categories as anyone, and second in that they search for love in wrong forms and places. The Crosbys, in seeing the non-unionized, anti-Communist Monzano regime as a sign of love for Americans, and in identifying those target figures of Marx, Mao, Castro, Stalin and Hitler as " 'practically every enemy that freedom ever had' " (p. 155), make both mistakes.

Jonah's wanting to have all of Mona's love, to stop her *boko-maruing* with other people, makes a related commentary. Once again, the episode is a comic one, and cannot be treated as a solemn propounding of moral thesis. Yet, with the aid of the context the whole novel provides, and of the immediate context supplied by the contrast between Mona's beautiful serenity and Jonah's grunting sex, a point is made: things might be better with more universal goodwill and less egocentric possessiveness. The other portrait of love in the novel involves the Mintons. They have the perfect *duprass,* and their absorption with each other seems almost total. In spite of what Bokonon says about a *duprass*' not being invaded even by offspring, Minton's grief over his son's death seems deep, and their awareness of the importance of love in the world about them has been mentioned. They may have accepted the fact of hate too readily, however, in retreating into their private world of love. The way in which they sail down to their deaths, hand-in-hand and smiling amiably, shows the sufficiency of their love, but also suggests the degree to which such an alliance may involve resignation from the world.

In short, *Cat's Cradle* implies values and limitations of love essentially similar to those expressed more directly in *The Sirens of Titan* and *Mother Night*. They are never as positively nor convincingly asserted, however, and never achieve the stature to counterbalance the existential void as they do in *The Sirens of Titan,* nor even to meet it as in *Mother Night*. That failure might be explained simply by the fact that, in its different way, *Cat's Cradle* is more pessimistic even than *Mother Night*, or that to do so would be to violate the form of the novel. In the earlier novels the consequences of life in a meaningless world are registered in terms of human feeling: the countering affirmations are supported in the same way. In *Cat's Cradle* these techniques of the representational novel are abandoned. At the conclusion there is no affirmative denouement, yet the horror of a bleak situation remains unreal, too. Instead there is a restatement of form, with Jonah looking for the "right symbol" to take to the mountain top, asking Newt what is supposed to be in his hands. We have a good idea what, but for the interruption of their seeing Bokonon, Newt might suggest.

So the ending reminds us again that we are in a fiction, that this is all a literary game. We do not actually *know* the ending, in the sense that we expect to as we close a representational novel. We only know what Bokonon suggests *he* would do, and that Bokonon always lies and says that no one should take his advice! It would be hard to count how many stages away from "reality" we are by that time—and it really does not matter. The end of Bokonon's book is the end of Jonah's is the end of Vonnegut's. Artifice upon artifice.

Within the dimensions of its chosen form, *Cat's Cradle* seems remarkably consistent and to work well. It might be the most popular of Vonnegut's novels among the young—such impressions are difficult to verify—and if it were that would not be hard to understand. To "the counter-culture" it should appeal as a book which counters almost every aspect of the culture of our society. To a generation which delights in the "put on," parody and artifice, often as the most meaningful expressions of deeply held convictions in a world which they see as prone to distortion, *Cat's Cradle*'s play with language, symbol and artifice should find accord. On the other hand, the novel somehow lacks the substance of the two which precede it. Compared with them, the plot remains rather thin, the characterizations are more superficial and often fragmentary, and the reader's involvement with characters, moral issues and human emotions is consequently shallower. The first person narration, which in *Mother Night* serves to further our involvement, fails to bring us appreciably closer to its speaker or the other characters. Part protagonist, part narrator-commentator, Jonah remains rather indistinct in both roles. It can also be argued that as a comedy, *Cat's Cradle* hardly fulfills its cathartic purpose by encountering the terrors of the world as we know them. Or that by failing to build sufficient tension between the threats which oppress us and the laughter which dissolves them, it remains essentially an entertainment. To make such judgment might be to take the novel too solemnly, or to discount its form—even its intentions. Conversely, it might be the fairest way to take those things into account, a way to give honest recognition to the merits and shortcomings of *Cat's Cradle*, and the possibilities and limitations of this form of novel.

V

Money and Madness:
God Bless You, Mr. Rosewater

Although this novel declares its subject and central character to be money, *God Bless You, Mr. Rosewater* (1965) concerns itself with a great deal more than that. Most obviously, the focus on money leads into considerations of the society that it makes run, into commentaries on class, social values, public morality, art, economics and politics. The next step is to probe the influences of money and the society on the lives of individuals; the psychological and moral consequences of both having and not having money. For money is not simply the root of all evil in the world of this novel. More importantly, it is the root of all neurosis. And neuroses abound to the extent that hardly a single character either is not or has not been afflicted psychologically in some way. Graffiti, the expression of troubled souls, comes close to being to this novel what the calypsos and poems of Bokonon are to *Cat's Cradle*. It is a world in which madness commonly passes as the standard for sanity, and where sanity appears neurotic. In effect, the novel comes almost as close to re-posing the question of "Hamlet's Madness" as it playfully suggests, as well as recasting the "To be or not to be" quandary in a contemporary rotten state. The nature of love, also a thematic problem in *Hamlet* and a subject Vonnegut constantly returns to, reemerges as a major consideration in this work. But *God Bless You, Mr. Rosewater* is no tragedy. Tragic events and tragic circumstances provide the element of pain that we expect of this dark humorist, but the novel stands as solid comedy and one of Vonnegut's funniest books.

God Bless You, Mr. Rosewater opens with the declaration that its subject and its leading character is *money*— to be specific $87,472,003.61. That amount constitutes the Rosewater fortune on June 1, 1964, placed in a foundation on the advice of McAllister, senior partner of McAllister, Robjent, Reed, and McGee. As the Rosewater Foundation, the money escapes taxation. The Presidency of the Foundation passes down in direct line of succession like a monarchy while the younger siblings of the President automatically become officers of the foundation, and all are free to draw as large salaries as they wish. The fortunes of the Foundation are administered by the Rosewater Corporation. The Corporation's executives cannot control what the Foundation's officers do with the profits, and the Foundation's officers cannot tell the Corporation's executives how to make the profits. The only potential serpent in this Garden of Eden is that the eldest heir can be excluded as chief beneficiary if he is proved insane.

Norman Mushari, a young assistant to McAllister, begins to dream of introducing that serpent into the monetary Paradise. This rapacious young Lebanese has learned above all from his training at Cornell Law School that when large sums of money change hands, a sharp

147

lawyer can make sure that some of it ends in his pocket. Mushari yearns to prove Eliot Rosewater, the current President of the Foundation, insane; and his chances of doing so seem good.

One of Mushari's pieces of evidence is a letter Eliot has written to whoever should succeed him, explaining the origins of the Rosewater fortune. It recounts the story from Noah Rosewater who bought a substitute in the Civil War, made a fortune by supplying the Federal forces, and swindled his blinded war-hero brother, on down to Lister Rosewater's putting the money in a foundation with Eliot as President. Eliot's admission of his drinking problem looks promising to Mushari, but the most convincing evidence of Eliot's madness is his admonition to his successor to be "a sincere, attentive friend of the poor."

Eliot, now 46, was educated at Loomis and Harvard, served with distinction in World War II, suffered combat fatigue, was invalided to Paris where he met Sylvia DuVrais Zetterling, married her, and returned to New York to run the Foundation. Between 1947 and 1953 he ran the Foundation flawlessly, spending $14 million of its money on such things as art treasures and medical research. But then Eliot began to crack, to drink increasingly, and finally disappeared for a week during which he attended a science fiction writers' convention and took up with volunteer firemen. He returned, underwent a seeming cure, but then gave way to a sudden outburst during a performance of *Aïda*.

Once again he flees New York, writing to Sylvia identifying himself with Hamlet and her with Ophelia, once more obsessed with volunteer firemen. Eventually he goes to the old family home of Rosewater, Indiana, where Sylvia joins him. They offend the young executive set of suburban Avondale, and devote themselves to helping Rosewater's poor. In time, however, Sylvia has a breakdown and, after treatment, leaves to resume her old life in Paris. A second breakdown follows, and divorce proceedings begin.

Eliot, meanwhile, has set up in a shabby one-room office-cum-dormitory in Rosewater as notary public, volunteer fireman, alcoholic and friend of the poor. "Rosewater Foundation, How Can We Help You?" provides both the motto on his door and his first words in answering the telephone. It now emerges that the source of Eliot's obsession with fire and volunteer firemen, and the cause of his original "battle-fatigue," was an episode during the war in which he led an attack into a burning building which was believed to be filled with S. S. troops. After Eliot had killed three Germans, he discovered that they were not S. S. troops but volunteer firemen—two old men and a fourteen year old boy—and he went into shock.

As Eliot goes on dispensing aspirins and wine, Ex-lax, small sums of money and encouragement to the poor and depressed people who call on him, his father, Senator Lister Rosewater, frets about the divorce and the consequences to the Foundation. After a long consultation with McAllister and Sylvia, and a phone conversation with Eliot, the Senator succeeds in arranging a meeting between husband and wife in Indianapolis.

We now shift to another line of the Rosewater family, the branch on which Mushari's plans depend. Fred and Caroline Rosewater live in Pisquontuit, Rhode Island, where Fred makes a marginal living as an insurance salesman while Caroline tries to escape her aversion to not being rich in alcoholism and the friendship of a wealthy lesbian named Amanita Buntline. The Buntlines present another study in wealth, their forebears having made a fortune by exploiting disabled Civil War veterans and by carpet-bagging. Now, at 40, Stewart Buntline is bored with sex, hobbies, and even alcohol, spending most of his days sleeping, his social conscience long dead. Amanita spends money on the junk antiques and overpriced lunches at the establishment of Bunny Weeks. An attraction of Bunny's restaurant is that with the supplied opera glasses guests can watch the activities of Harry Pena and his sons as they haul in their fishing nets. Coarse and hale, Harry is the most lifeful person in a listless town. Mushari arrives in Pisquontuit after a diversion to visit the Rumfoord Estate, just in time to save Fred Rosewater from suicide.

149

Eliot's preparations for the meeting in Indianapolis are disturbed by the arrival of his father. The father berates the town drunk, rails at the squalor of Eliot's quarters, and reveals again his neurotic aversion to pubic hair, but otherwise gets on quite well with his son. Until, that is, Eliot mentions the word which the Senator feels he has profaned—"love." Lister raves that Eliot is in no position to talk of love, considering how he has shown love to his father and to his wife. The outburst jolts Eliot into a state of shock. A local ex-convict diagnoses Eliot's condition as "the click"—the point where what ever has been the driving motivation within a person suddenly dies.

Eliot blunders out of Rosewater, not recognizing those he has helped for years. He takes the bus to Indianapolis, reading a novel by Kilgore Trout, his favorite science fiction writer, as he goes. When he looks up from his book to see Indianapolis, his perception of the city becomes fused with a vision of the firestorm precipitated by the bombing of Dresden. He sees Indianapolis in flames—and then all goes black.

When the blackness lifts, Eliot finds himself in the garden of a private mental hospital. Somehow he has lost a year during which he has received treatment, played tennis, and become to all appearances fit and sane again. With him are his father, McAllister, and Kilgore Trout, who are preparing him for the next day's sanity hearings being brought by Mushari for the Pisquontuit Rosewaters. Trout's idea is that Eliot claim to have been conducting social experiments in how to love, and to make feel loved, people who in a technological society no longer have any purpose. The talk also turns to the fact that, bribed by Mushari, a variety of Rosewater County women have brought fifty-seven paternity cases against Eliot. These are all baseless and stand no chance in court, but their mention brings Eliot's memory flooding back. If he had an heir, there would be neither need nor grounds for the sanity hearing. Accordingly, Eliot writes a check for $100,000 to Fred Rosewater, and then instructs that the rest of his estate be distributed among the fifty-seven supposed bastards, with the commandment " 'be fruitful and multiply.' "

Any summary of *God Bless You, Mr. Rosewater* does the novel a disservice. It is one of those novels which we are likely to describe to friends by recounting episode or insight rather than be recalling plot. Not that the plot should be called inadequate; it may be digressive and episodic, but it generally coheres and it holds our interest. Even so, the plot remains primarily a vehicle—a well developed and self supporting vehicle—for the questions and theses of the novel. Rather the same judgment might be reached on the characterization. There are gaps in the depiction of Eliot Rosewater, and other characters such as Norman Mushari, Sylvia and Senator Rosewater are only partially realized. We sense that these characters are *used* rather than *are*. Yet they do come to life, engaging us emotionally. As its opening suggests, the novel makes a sum of money "a leading character." In fact, money and its ramifications become more important than character and plot, but these are well served, and the book achieves a balance between its large purpose of social criticism and its development as narrative.

This novel's rationale is effectively written by its own central character. When Eliot Rosewater attends the science fiction writers' convention, he wonders why no good science fiction book has ever been written about money. " 'Just think of the wild ways money is passed around on Earth!' he said." Nor need we look to Tralfamadore for creatures with incredible powers. " 'Look at the powers of an Earthling millionaire! Look at me!' " (p. 21). *God Bless You, Mr. Rosewater* does look at the wild ways money is passed around, at the powers of a millionaire, and at Eliot Rosewater. It looks at the other side of the coin—or the Rosewater fortune—as well. And it does not simply castigate the "haves" for being rich or for the ways they came by wealth, and plead the case of the "have nots" or the pathos of their having not. It probes the burdens that can attend wealth, the problems that can accompany giving to the poor, and more than these, it exposes the inversions of values and loss of purpose that can afflict a society which esteems its currency above its people. In short, it shows money as a sort of psychological germ-carrier, afflicting both collective and individual man.

Eliot's history of the Rosewater fortune, although obviously not an unbiased record, is one of the several indicators of the distortion of social values which comes in the wake of wealth. Eliot theorizes that an error of the Founding Fathers was in putting no limit on the riches of each citizen, out of the misconception that the resources of the continent were infinite, more than enough for everyone. Men like his forefather Noah exploited this omission, grabbing and bribing their ways to wealth. "Thus did a handful of rapacious citizens come to control all that was worth controlling in America. Thus was the savage and stupid and entirely inappropriate and unnecessary and humorless American class system created" (p. 12). In this system, hardworking men who asked for living wages were "classed as bloodsuckers," while riches went to those subtle enough to commit "crimes against which no laws had been passed." And in this system, continues Eliot, "every grotesquely rich American represents property, privileges, and pleasures that have been denied the many" (p. 13). For Noah Rosewater and his ilk, who acquire out of a "paranoid reluctance to be a victim," Eliot contrives two appropriate mottos: *"Grab much too much, or you'll get nothing at all,"* and: *"Anybody who thought that the United States of America was supposed to be a Utopia was a piggy, lazy, God-damned fool"* (p. 13). Thus the distortion of a potential Utopia into a nightmare land of possessiveness, greed and insecurity. While all of these opinions are ascribed only to Eliot, they deserve reviewing for what they tell us about the protagonist and because they express, by and large, the attitudes adopted by the novel itself.

The early Rosewaters are not the only ones who have come by their money through dubious means and warped ethics. The Buntline fortune began when Castor Buntline set up a broom-making factory employing blind Civil War veterans, cynically recognizing that such men would make compliant workers, that he would be acknowledged as a humanitarian, and that people would buy the brooms out of patriotism. Both early Buntlines and early Rosewaters are unscrupulous in their money making, but are equally fond of Bible quoting and moral preaching. The men who make these great fortunes, goaded by the insecurity which demands more and more, were not simply crooks. Ironically, they could know they were crooks and yet be sanctimonious at the same time. The perversion that comes down to the present generation is that they no longer recognize themselves as crooks to any degree, but are more sanctimonious than ever. Lister Rosewater appears to be one of those Republicans Eliot refers to as being willing to "order the militia to fire into crowds whenever a poor man seemed on the point of suggesting that he and Rosewater were equal in the eyes of the law" (p. 13). He advocates a return to "a true Free Enterprise system" with "sink-or-swim justice," where the swimmers triumph and the others sink quietly away (pp. 24-27). The moral line of the Buntlines emphasizes the sanctity of property rather more. It is epitomized in the oath, written by Castor Buntline, which the inmates of the orphanage he has endowed must recite nightly: "I do solemnly swear that I will respect the sacred private property of others, and that I will be content with whatever station in life God Almighty may assign me to. . ." (p. 133).

This is the mentality which defends that "unnecessary and humorless American class system," the characteristics of which emerge repeatedly in the novel. One instance can be seen in the "inner city" and suburban split between Rosewater and Avondale. Rosewater has the high school, the city park, the fire department, and that is about all, since the Saw Company has moved out to a commercial park. Its working class citizenry has become an idle class. Meanwhile, "the few highly paid agronomists, engineers, brewers, accountants, and administrators who did all that needed doing lived in a defensive circle of expensive ranch homes" in Avondale (p. 39). Once these people have observed with contempt the decline of the Rosewater aristocracy, their self-esteem rises: they see themselves not as rising young executives but as the "vigorous members of the true ruling class" (p. 41). As in *Player Piano*, a technological managerial class emerges as the new aristocracy—and it is just as shallow and crass. Meanwhile the "working class" becomes redundant and rejected in another enclave. Thus does a national schizophrenia become manifest in both social and geographical division. Pisquontuit shows the same split personality, being "populated by two hundred very wealthy families and by a thousand ordinary families whose breadwinners served, in one way and another, the rich" (p. 96). Then there are the Rumfoords living in magnificent isolation in their Newport estate. They are required to open their domain to the public once every five years by the will of a forefather who thought it would be to their benefit to catch an occasional glimpse of some of the world's inhabitants. Mrs. Rumfoord indicates the success of the program when she insists that Mushari, whom we are told is prone to see everything as if through a quart of olive oil, had been a sniper in the U. S. Infantry. And so the phobias of wealth pile up.

The American class system, the novel argues, in effect institutionalizes money. Like most class systems its function is to protect its aristocracy and keep its masses contentedly, respectfully and industriously in their places. The American aristocracy may have bought itself refinement in successive generations, but it remains essentially an aristocracy of money. Its original power came from money gained by ruthless acquisitiveness, and the laws and ethics it has propagated have been devoted to preserving that power. The law should ensure the protection of property and the perpetuation of an environment in which egalitarianism is not encouraged. It should curb pressures for such things as higher wages, but not block the tax-evading shenanigans of the rich. The ethic teaches that hard work is a virture to be accompanied by respect for one's betters (or richers) and contentment with place. To be unwilling or unable to work is sinful. Unless one is rich. But then, of course, the ethic assures that riches never come undeservedly, so the rich deserve to be idle. To be rich means to have one's intelligence and value assured. To be poor implies one is stupid, inferior and valueless. While not very much of all this is new with Vonnegut, his explanations of the social and personal consequences of such a system are penetrating and relevant, particularly in showing the effects upon rich as well as poor. Moreover, Vonnegut does bring new emphasis to the impact of technological displacement upon a nation reared with the work ethic. Above all, his attention to the psychological imbalance that derives such a system, and to the neuroses engendered by it, is fresh and emphatic.

All of these implications of *money* are best demonstrated in the specific. Eliot Rosewater is naturally the one character on whom the moral questions imposed by wealth settle most heavily. His likening of himself to Shakespeare's Hamlet means more than his being the heir in a rotten state. Like Hamlet he faces questions that could drive him mad, like Hamlet his most sane behavior might well appear crazy in a world of inverted values, and like Hamlet he has received a psychological blow which could indeed have unbalanced him. The great shock for Eliot has been that wartime experience in which he mistook volunteer firemen for S. S. troops and killed three innocent men. This prompts his obsession with the propensity of things to combine with oxygen and be consumed, and his passion for volunteer firemen. It also explains at least one of his "crazy" outbursts, contributes to his later breakdowns and to his drinking. But it also has sharpened his conscience, has given him a peculiar insight into man's overwhelming responsibilities to other men, and could have revealed to him, if only subconsciously, the symbol of volunteer fireman as helper of men which Trout suggests later. Consequently the possibility exists, not just for his detractors but for the detached observer, that Eliot's social conscience and actions are a result of that shock and can be judged unbalanced, just as the probable prior existence of an Oedipal complex adds ambiguity to Hamlet's response to the death of

155

his father. That touch of ambiguity greatly enriches the novel. It adds dimension to Eliot's characterization, makes the social criticism exercised through his role less easily propagandistic, and connects the cold subject of money directly with very real human sufferings.

From the start, Eliot's concern with the poor and with the inequitable distribution of wealth is not solely altruistic. One might dispute whether action to relieve the naggings of conscience represents altruism or egocentrism, but in any case conscience works on Eliot, as does a sense of purposelessness. That dissatisfaction creeps through the ironies of the last paragraph of his letter to his heir as he says, " 'Be generous. Be kind. You can safely ignore the arts and sciences. They never helped anybody. Be a sincere, attentive friend of the poor' " (p. 15). Eliot means both that the arts and sciences never helped others—that pouring money into museums and research institutions will give the poor little relief—and that they never really helped the rich donor, either. As he recites on one of those earlier days of running the Foundation:

"Many, many good things have I bought!
Many, many bad things have I fought!" (p. 17)

The bad things include alcoholism, but he is too drunk himself to read the report on it that he has commissioned. Eliot obviously finds no real purpose, and certainly not enough human contact, in playing the philanthropic mogul.

Those first alcoholic, emotionally distraught junkets that Eliot goes on all point to a search for meaning and purpose. Eliot's seizing upon science fiction writers as the seers of the contemporary world is fraught with comic undercutting, but shows clearly the method in his madness. What he loves about science fiction writers, Eliot says, is that they are the only ones aware of the changes going on around men who care about the future; about what machines, cities, big simple solutions, mistakes, accidents, and catastrophies do to people (p. 18). In the latter part of this, we may see the results of the war trauma working on Eliot, but its application to the general condition of men lacks no logic. In particular, Eliot praises Kilgore Trout for his book *2BRO2B,* a title which casts Hamlet's famous question in new symbols. Trout's novel examines the problems Eliot has alluded to, of life in an automated America where there is no work for people with less than three Ph.D.s, where there are serious overpopulation problems, "Ethical Suicide Parlors" next to every Howard Johnson's, and a general sense of purposelessness. One character voices the question that plagues Eliot, and which echoes through Vonnegut: " 'What in hell are people *for*?' " (p. 21).

The two questions, "2BRO2B," and "What are people for?" are connected for Eliot as well as for others. Finding some purpose resolves the question of being. The rub comes in finding the purpose, and that becomes Eliot's search. He writes to his "Dear Ophelia"—Sylvia—from Elsinore, California, that he feels he has an important mission but cannot decide how it should be done (hence his Hamlet complex). Hamlet, he feels, had "one big edge" on him, in having a father's ghost to tell him exactly what to do. But Eliot's instinct for firemen leads him in the right direction. As Trout says near the novel's close, volunteer firemen rush to the rescue of any and all human beings without counting the cost, making them the perfect symbol of "enthusiastic unselfishness." What Eliot tries to do in setting up his rescue service in Rosewater obviously parallels a volunteer firebrigade. His two telephones, a red one for fire calls and a black one for humans about to be consumed, emphasizes the parallel. So does the William Blake poem he has painted on the stairs to his office, proclaiming the message so loved by Gulley Jimson of Joyce Cary's *The Horse's Mouth*: " 'Go love without the help of any thing on Earth' " (p. 51).

"ROSEWATER FOUNDATION. HOW CAN WE HELP YOU?" asks the sign on Eliot's door. The question might almost have been written in response to the name, for Eliot seems as desperately in need of help as most of his clients. But what he does in Rosewater is creditable in deed as well as intention, and makes more sense than his earlier gestures of inviting derelicts off the street to lavish dinners in the Rosewater mansion. His activities are not always the pattern of rationality, and they receive their full share of undercutting. His prescriptions—a glass of wine and an aspirin—and his therapy—organized fly hunts—are often ludicrous, as are his personal appearance and, frequently, his manner. He is even shown to be excessively romantic in his conception of his clients. Senator Rosewater and McAllister may be wrong in their judgment that he "trafficked with criminals," but Eliot "was almost equally mistaken" in taking his following for people like those who "had cleared the forests, drained the swamps, built the bridges, people whose sons formed the backbone of the infantry in time of war—and so on" (p. 56). In fact, we are told, they are both "weaker"and more "dumb" than such people. Those closer to Eliot's description eschew his assistance and try, all too often unsuccessfully, to find work to support themselves. Even the idealism of Eliot's quotation is countered by another from the same poet, scribbled on the hall wall by the Senator:

Love seeketh only Self to please,
To bind another to Its delight,
Joys in another's loss of ease,
And builds a Hell in Heaven's despite. (p. 52)

That poem seems hilarious in context—the Senator sees his son as delighting in the loss of ease, and certainly views the chaotic office as a Hell built in Heaven's despite—but it also points more seriously to the dangers of egocentrism in Eliot's program.

For all the derision and farce surrounding it, Eliot's rescue service has obvious merits. He may be romantically unrealistic about the heritage of the people he serves, and much of his comforting may be as "hopelessly sentimental" as the music of rainfall which on occasion tellingly accompanies it (p. 60), but he gives "uncritical love" and is not devoid of all practical sense. His remedies, for instance, do not involve the unquestioning distribution of large sums of money, which would surely be the gesture of a man simply trying to assuage feelings of guilt about his own wealth. Giving money generally remains his last resort, and then he will haggle about how much. Nor is he without a sense of humor about what he does, as he shows in the telephone conversation with an anonymous potential suicide. After some verbal exchange, the caller decides Eliot sounds drunk and demands, " 'Who the hell *are* you?' " Eliot replies that if he wants to keep people from killing themselves and he is not a Church, he must be either the Government or the Community Chest (p. 76). Joke or not, crazy or not, Eliot gives unstintingly of himself, extends compassion to many who need it and succeeds in making life more bearable for a number of people. In *form* his program may not offer the best solution to the problems of inequities in the distribution of wealth, but it springs from the right principles.

The real measure of Eliot's behavior and sanity is provided in the way other characters' actions are juxtaposed to his. Foremost among these yardstick characters are Norman Mushari, Senator Rosewater, and, to a lesser degree, Stewart Buntline. The obvious basis of contrast between Eliot and Mushari is that the former has wealth, a conscience, and a distaste for acquisitiveness, while the latter has no wealth, no conscience, but great greed. Without question the descriptive odds are stacked against Mushari from the start. He stands only five feet three inches tall. Short stature is not necessarily pejorative in Vonnegut, but combine it with his posterior of excessive proportions, his lack of wit, his being tone-deaf, and the fact that his office fellows whistle "Pop Goes the Weasel" as he passes, and we have a clear enough picture. He salivates at the thought of money, and at a moment when she is grieved gives Sylvia "a hideously inappropriate smile of greed and fornication" p. 54). On top of that his boyhood idols are Senator Joe McCarthy and Roy Cohn. Actually, making Mushari a political conservative seems almost gratuitous. There is little else in his characterization to support his political affinities, except in so far as the novel does align the right-wing of the Republican party with the "God helps those who help themselves to everybody else's" mentality. Mushari's reading *The Conscience of a Conservative* seems rather ironic, in fact, since he has no conscience and is more acquisitive than conservative. There again the connection lies in the play on Goldwater/ Rosewater and the satire of the right wing. Mushari's inspiration is a lecture by his favorite law professor which explains that in every money transaction there comes a moment when the booty has been surrendered by the original owner but not yet received by the new one. That is an astute lawyer's magic moment. " 'If the man who is to receive the treasure is unused to wealth, has an inferiority complex and shapeless feelings of guilt, as most people do, the lawyer can often take as much as half the bundle, and still receive the recipient's blubbering thanks' " (p. 9). To that end, Mushari will try to ensure a divorce between two loving people and will work to prove a man insane. Measured against this young lawyer's calculated schemes, Eliot's earlier outbursts and irrationalities seem both human and moral, and ultimately more "sane." Incidentally, once Mushari has provided that contrast with Eliot, he fades rapidly in the novel, after having been introduced as if he would be a major character. Subsequently his role becomes only a plot convenience, connecting the Pisquontuit Rosewaters with the main narrative and providing the threat of Eliot's sanity hearing.

Senator Lister Rosewater's importance grows as Mushari's fades. For all that his politics are essentially cruel and his values often warped, the Senator becomes an almost endearing character. We can well understand why even when suffering his insults Kilgore Trout can enjoy the senior Rosewater for what he is. Even in his "Golden Age of Rome" speech, a classic expression of right-wing paranoia, he somehow emerges more as buffoon than as threat (pp. 24-27). His ability to laugh at himself and at the image others have of him, his bluster, and the sheer physical force that emanates from his characterization, all lend him some appeal. We also sense that in his domineering way he genuinely does love Eliot and Sylvia. (As a caring father he contrasts with Felix Hoenikker and even

160

with the fathers of Paul Proteus and Malachi Constant.)
His social conscience, however, is registered when he
speaks of Eliot's activities among his constituents. " 'In
his heart. . .' " he says, in a negative echo of Barry Goldwater, " 'Eliot doesn't love those people out there any
more than I do. . . If Eliot's booze were shut off, his compassion for the maggots in the slime on the bottom of the
human garbage pail would vanish' " (p. 46). For the
Senator, garbage, slime, or anything other than good clean
wholesome living is anathema. To his credit, he does say
that he has never thought much about perversion because
there never seemed much in it to think about—a reaction
which we might, like the psychiatrist, find healthier than
we expected. But his embarrassment by naked bodies and
his aversion to pubic hair seem less healthy. They even
afford him a specific definition of pornography: it is anything which calls attention to reproductive organs, dis-
charges, or bodily hair. " 'The difference between
pornography and art is bodily hair!' " (p. 72). In short,
the Senator indulges in a form of superiority complex in
which dirt, hair, sex, fat and inebriation are all seen as
aspects of the lower orders of life which he holds in contempt.

The contrast between father and son extends further
than one's being dirty, drunk, fat, and intrigued by his own
pubic hair and the other's being averse to all these things.
(Lister Rosewater has a hygienic mouthwash-cum-cologne
sound to it, although the Senator is strictly a soap and
water man.) It comes down to the fact that Eliot cares for
people, accepts their variety, their weakness, their physi-
cality, and is troubled by their suffering, while his father
cares little for the mass of human kind and regards most
deprivations as deserved. Like the two Blake poems they
quote, they represent contrasting aspects of love. Having
experienced the consequences of hate and of plain error,
Eliot sets himself the awesome task of simply loving without reserve and without help. Lister is also capable of love,
but of the individualized, selective and possessive variety.
He can love his son or Sylvia, but is appalled by Eliot's
general love because it lacks "discrimination." His quota-

tion suggests he sees Eliot's love as the kind which "seeketh only Self to please," as a self-indulgence. Ironically, Blake's phrase aptly describes Lister's love, in that by discriminating between those he judges deserve it and those who do not, he makes his love self-pleasing. Yet there is some support for his charge against Eliot. The psychiatrist suggests that Eliot has "his wires crossed" so that all his sexual energies are directed toward an "inappropriate" object—Utopia (p. 73).

At this point we can see how the subjects of love and money intersect. Lister is possessive of money, people, and love, wanting his money to go to those he loves, people who are *his*. Eliot takes the reverse tack, wanting to distribute wealth and love among all people. The capitalistic father sees the free distribution of money and love as indiscriminate, devaluing and contrary to his ethic that both things should be deserved. The egalitarian son feels all men inherently merit their share of both, and regards the hoarding of wealth and the withholding of love from one's fellows as mutually supporting vices. He also recognizes the corrupting influence of money and avoids the mistake of regarding it as an answer to all problems. The novel vindicates Eliot, but not without reservations. As mentioned earlier, the Senator is not made simply unloving, and some of Eliot's performances of love are ludicrous. His distaste for what money does to people leads Eliot into a neurotic wallowing in self-neglect. And Lister's condemnation of the way Eliot has shown love to his father and to the woman "whose only fault had been to love him" hits home. Rather like the song from *Hair* which asks how "people who care about strangers" can be cruel to those they love, it makes the point that universal compassion can blind people to the responsibilities of personal love as easily as a "nation of two" can be an evasion of wider human concern. Eliot tries to shut out the words, but cannot avoid their truth. Thus begins his last great breakdown.

Stewart Buntline has a lesser but still important role as a figure who contrasts with Eliot. He can be seen as representing what Eliot could have become. In his younger days, he too has been disturbed by the notion that he has so much while others have so little. He goes to McAllister, who guides Buntlines as well as Rosewaters, and says that he has more money than he needs and that he wants to use it to end some of the world's sufferings, buying food, clothing and housing for the poor. For McAllister this is a familiar line. Numerous young men come to him with the same story. McAllister's argument is simple: a great fortune is a miracle to be learned about and treasured; it is what makes the rich man important in his own as well as others' eyes; without that fortune he would be less happy and free; without it he would be nothing, his descendants would suffer and would regard him as a fool who "piddled a fortune away." Money, McAllister concludes, is "dehydrated Utopia," a miracle that can make life a paradise (pp. 119-121). Stewart yields to this, but the paradise he assumes is indeed dehydrated. At forty-odd he is "through with misguided pity," through with sex, through even with his hobby of Civil War history, and spends most of his day sleeping with an untouched Scotch and soda by his side. He becomes so inert that his daughter always checks as she passes to be sure he is not literally dead. Once again, the man who follows the system looks singularly unhealthy in comparison with the "sick" Eliot. On the symbolic scale, Buntline, looking like death and "through with sex," is weighed against Rosewater who at the end plays tennis like a champion and acknowledges fifty-seven "heirs."

Sterility, perversion, or having "wires crossed" so that sexual energies are misdirected—as the psychiatrist says of Eliot—become familiar symptoms in the world of this novel. In Pisquontuit the tone is set by the passing around of *The American Investigator,* with its advertisements for male hairdressers and swinging couples who want to exchange photographs, executives who want weekday afternoon dates with non-prudes, and prep-school teachers looking for stern Teutonic horse-loving instructresses. Peopling this scene are the suicidal Fred Rosewater, furtively sneaking peeks at sex magazines; his wife Caroline who is drunk after lunch daily; Amanita Buntline, a

163

kultchur-vulture lesbian; her daughter Lila, who at thirteen pedals pornography to other children at high profit; and Bunny Weeks, a homosexual who runs a restaurant and gift shop. By midafternoon, by the way, all of these people seem to be asleep. The liveliest ones in Pisquontuit are the fisherman Harry Pena and his two sons.

As Harry's last name perhaps too obviously suggests, he stands for virility, fertility and life. He is surrounded by fish and sea, in case we need more symbols, and tells Fred that the picture of a French girl in a bikini is not a woman but ink on paper. "If this was a real girl, all I'd have to do for a living would be to stay home and cut out pictures of big fish" (p. 109). Hale, hearty and earthy, Harry Pena becomes a rather romantic and sentimentalized characterization, but he serves a useful function in emphasizing through contrast the aridity and neurosis of the rest of Pisquontuit. His story counterpoints those of Bunny Weeks, Stewart and Amanita, Fred and Caroline, and of Mushari's visit to the Rumfoords. While Harry fishes for "real fish" with his "two real sons" in "a real boat on a salty sea" (p. 111), all else in Pisquontuit is artifice. The homosexual Bunny Weeks gaily paws his female customers, sells seventeen-dollar toilet roll covers and other gimcrackery in his shop or hands out opera glasses so that his restaurant customers can watch the activities of the fishermen. (Caroline watches them and says " 'It's so much like life.' ") Fred Rosewater dreams the afternoon away in his boat, his only consolation the knowledge that when he dies his widow will receive a healthy insurance benefit. Caroline apes Amanita and drinks away her aversion to not living in the style to which she would like to be accustomed. Amanita patronizes Caroline, spends money, patronizes the orphan Selena, spends money, plays Beethoven records at the wrong speed, adores the taste of Bunny Weeks and *Better Homes and Gardens,* and spends money. Stewart sleeps.

The two camps are mutually contemptuous of each other. As the fishermen take the mighty fish, they swear and laugh and feel full of joy. "All three were as satisfied with life as man can ever be. The youngest boy thumbed his nose at the fairy's restaurant. 'Fuck 'em all, boys. Right?' said Harry" (p. 130). In the restaurant, Bunny judges that the " 'three romantics out there make as much sense as Marie Antoinette and her milkmaids' " (p. 131). Men like that, he says, working with their hands and backs, are not needed any more. They are losing everywhere. Yet with equal contempt, Bunny looks at his fat customers who have all inherited, and at himself who is making money, and says, " 'And look who's winning. And look who's won' " (p. 131). The terrible truth in his comments is that men like Harry are a dying breed, and the number who can find purpose and satisfaction in labor continues to dwindle in an automated America. The irony is that the loser feels happy while the man who is winning and those who have won feel only boredom and resentment. But Harry and his boys are practically unique in this novel, and they too are being hunted down by money since, as Bunny reveals, they are going broke.

The overall portrayal of society in *God Bless You, Mr. Rosewater,* is of a sick, sterile wasteland. Hardly a character appears who has not either a psychological or physical ailment. The pathetic Diana Moon Glampers believes the lightning is out to kill her and suffers constantly from psychosomatic kidney pains, while the seemingly prospering Fire Chief Charley Warmergran has the "fatal flaw" of not believing that he does have gonorrhea. Until debt catches up with him, at least, Harry Pena appears the one exception, and he derives a sense of purpose from natural outdoor work. There are two conclusions to be drawn from this portrayal of society, and Kilgore Trout —another of Vonnegut's portraits of the artist—makes them both. One is that people need a sense of being for something, of some use or value, and that few of them find this. The second is that in such a world, where so many are afflicted and suffer, " 'people can use all the uncritical love they can get' " (p. 186). There might be a third point to be made—that much of the reason why love has been replaced by self-interest and indifference, and why meaning or purpose has been lost to rich and poor alike, stems from money.

Not surprisingly. Kilgore Trout's commentary on the loss of purpose in a technological world resembles that advanced in *Player Piano*. Machines have supplanted men as producers of goods and services, and are already in the process of doing so as sources of practical ideas in other fields like engineering, economics and medicine. This leaves an increasing number of people without a function, often without work at all. The American work ethic has taught hatred of people who will not or cannot work, and contempt for oneself in that same situation. Hence the conditions prevailing in Rosewater, where "the Senator's people" who try to work and to keep going themselves despise the welfare recipients and unemployables who gravitate to Eliot, who in turn despise themselves. The lower income echelons feel purposeless either because they have no work or because their work seems meaningless, providing neither satisfaction nor advancement. Senator Rosewater argues that people can still work their way "out of the mire." Trout acknowledges the truth of this, but points out that even so, they or their children are likely to end up " 'in a Utopia like Pisquontuit, where, I am sure, the soul-rot and the silliness and torpor and insensibility are exactly as horrible as anything epidemic in Rosewater County' " (p. 184). As for the rich, we have seen that their inherited wealth leaves them victim to the work ethic, too. Either they work to perpetuate their situation, like Lister, and suffer the moral consequences, or they feel the frustrated purposelessness of Eliot in trying to find a way to make their wealth work to alleviate suffering, or like Stewart they float on their wealth and find no purpose in anything.

As Trout says, " 'The problem is this: How to love people who have no use?' " The answer is to a find way of " 'treasuring human beings because they are *human beings*. . .' " (p. 183). And that, as he says, is not only rare, but difficult in practice. Volunteer firemen provide the model, in that they will aid, rescue and comfort any man regardless of his worth, esteem or wealth. Eliot's compulsion to aid and comfort the suffering and to rescue those on the brink of suicide is comparable. The break-

166

downs of Eliot and Sylvia demonstrate the difficulties of following such a course when it runs counter to the general direction of the society. Sylvia shares Eliot's concerns, and even after her second breakdown demonstrates that she believes in the rightness of what he is doing. Her collapses prove most informative in that they derive almost solely from the stresses of trying to aid the disadvantaged, whereas Eliot's are always complicated by the possibility of their being influenced by his war trauma. Her psychiatrist labels Sylvia's original illness "Samaritrophia," which he describes as " *hysterical indifference to the troubles of those less fortunate than oneself* " (p. 41). This state comes about when the conscience dominates the rest of the mind, until the other processes rebel, noting that the conscience is never satisfied nor the world ever improved by all the unselfish acts demanded. The other parts of the mind then reject the conscience, following instead Enlightened Self-Interest, whose motto is, "The hell with you, Jack, I've got mine!" (p. 42). The satire in this description, one might think, applies almost universally in our society. But it goes further. The majority of upperclass people in a prosperous, industrialized society, says the doctor, hardly ever hear their consciences at all. Thus he concludes that " 'samaritrophia is only a disease, and a violent one, too, when it attacks those exceedingly rare individuals who reach biological maturity still loving and wanting to help their fellow men' " (p. 43). Sylvia's reaction follows predictable lines: a complete silencing of conscience and a giving over to self-indulgence. But this, too, fails, and another breakdown follows, after which Sylvia emerges in a frail condition, obviously believing in the rightness of Eliot's concern but unable to withstand the rigors of the life it demands.

In the touching telephone conversation in which Sylvia agrees to meet Eliot one last time in Indianapolis, it becomes apparent without her making any direct appeal that she desperately needs and wants the love and support of her husband. That Eliot has been too obsessed with his crusade to give her the love she needs has been apparent, and that at heart he knows it is suggested when he breaks

167

down as the Senator accuses him of this neglect. As the psychiatrist tells the Senator, Eliot's sexual energies have been rechanneled into social reform. This diversion of sexual energy is emphasized in another, comic episode. Reading a pornographic novel by Arthur Garvey Ulm, a writer he had patronized years before, Eliot finds himself with an erection. " 'Oh, for heavens' sake,' he said to his procreative organ, 'how irrelevant can you be?' " And the immediately following paragraph begins with the Senator lamenting, " 'If only there had been a child' " (p. 70). It is a telling juxtaposition of lines in a novel where so much emphasis is placed on virility and on real men encountering real life as opposed to perversion, aridity, sterility and artifice. Eliot's erection is as irrelevant as Fred's leching over the bikinied damsel who is only paper and ink, but is also irrelevant in the sense that his procreative powers are miscast in the course he has chosen to follow. There appears to be a continuance of the idea expressed in *Cat's Cradle*, that where men see no purpose in existing the urge to reproduce fades or becomes perverted.

And so Eliot "clicks"—to use the term Noyes Finnerty coins. As Noyes describes it, this happens when a man who has been possessed of some irresistible motivation for years, some secret compulsion always driving him on, suddenly goes flat, empty, dead, that inner force spent forever (pp. 164-5). Why does this happen to Eliot? Because he has simply reached the end of his tether? Because his Rosewater project has run its course, with no further possibility of development and no ultimate satisfaction? Because of the charges of his father? Possibly it is because of all of these things. Certainly he has become increasingly strained, tired, alcoholic, and even cynical about himself. His father's words do provide the last straw, as if Eliot recognizes that his efforts may after all have been selfish or as though he realizes that even in trying to show love to so many he has neglected and hurt others he loves. His vision of the firestorm as he drives into Indianapolis tends to confirm this surmise. The Trout novel he is reading has just recounted the death of the Milky Way.

Eliot looks up to discover that "Rosewater County was gone. He did not miss it" (p. 174). That curious juxtaposition suggests Eliot has more than "samaritrophia," for next comes the Dresden-firestorm-in-Indianapolis, another sort of end of the world. When Dresden was bombed, Eliot recalls, high explosive bombs were dropped before the incendiaries to put the fire brigades out of action. Without them there was no one to counter the final conflagration. Eliot's vision, then, seems to be a manifestation of his perception of a world about to be consumed, about to combine with the oxygen of hate, indifference, greed, self-interest and purposelessness, with no "firemen" to save it. Perhaps he feels that, in the treatment of Sylvia that Lister charged him with, he has again killed firemen by mistake. Perhaps he feels that he, like the firemen of Dresden, has been bombed underground. Oh perhaps he is overcome by the hopelessness of the odds against which he struggles. What precisely goes on in his unconscious we are not told, but the general implications of his breakdown are plain enough. Having the sanity to feel compassion in such a world is enough to drive a man insane. So is trying to act on that feeling, and so is trying to make love work.

Hamlet's struggles to do the right thing perturb his father's spirit and drive the woman he loves mad. Eliot drives his father to distraction, and causes his wife two breakdowns which finally put her in a nunnery where "the rest is silence." Hamlet delays killing Claudius largely on moral scruples, but becomes responsible for the deaths of others and the madness of Ophelia. As Eliot sees things run their course in spite of his efforts, he might be tempted to conclude like Hamlet that "There's a divinity that shapes our ends,/Rough-hew them how we will." Hamlet surrenders to that inevitability, and goes to his tragic end. Eliot recovers from his breakdown, confused, uncertain, and looking, as he puts it, like " 'F. Scott Fitzgerald, with one day to live' " (p. 182). But his end is triumphant, if still in a rather crazy way. Eliot has not forced his conscience into an "oubliette," but has learned, or clung to, what Trout affirms as the greatest lesson to be gained from his experiment: " 'that people can use all the uncritical love they can get' " (p. 186). Or as Eliot himself puts it, " 'God damn it, you've got to be kind' " (p. 93): Eliot demonstrates his uncritical love by acknowledging all those spurious offspring as his heirs and by the message he sends them: " 'And tell them that their father loves them, no matter what they turn out to be. And tell them . . . to be fruitful and multiply' " (p. 190).

Once again Vonnegut moves to an ending that meets the requirements of comedy, dark as that comedy may be. The final note is affirmative, with the emphasis appropriately on fertility, love, abundance, and distribution of blessings—more like *A Midsummer Night's Dream* or *The Tempest* than *Hamlet*. Yet it remains something of a throwaway ending, with comic undercutting on the one hand and darkly tragic implications on the other. Eliot's solution—declaring heirs children who can be proven not to be his—is in effect nutty enough to substantiate the insanity charges it was designed to thwart. It provides a delightful twist to the ending—Eliot beating Mushari on a technicality—but it leaves troubling questions. Is there no way a man can follow his conscience without being judged mad or actually going mad in this society? Is there no more viable solution to the human sufferings, the inequalities, and the neuroses which afflict contemporary America? Is there no more substantial hope than this for the emergence of "uncritical love," for the "treasuring of human beings as *human beings*" in our society? Vonnegut's answer again comes through Kilgore Trout: " 'If one man can do it, perhaps others can do it too . . . Thanks to the example of Eliot Rosewater, millions and millions of people may learn to love and help whomever they see' " (p. 187). It sounds more like a prayer than an assurance.

The subtitle of the novel—*Or Pearls before Swine*—introduces the ambiguity which pervades *God Bless You, Mr. Rosewater*. Obviously it presents two ways of interpreting Eliot's actions, the title reflecting Diana Moon Glampers' response and the subtitle the view of Lister Rosewater. The subtitle is socially satirical, in that the kind of society the novel depicts would see the actions of this latter day Jesus-figure as "casting pearls before swine." It might also refer to the fact that in this society the rich get richer, the piggy acquisitors being the ones to whom more pearls are cast. And maybe Eliot's well-intentioned actions are as futile as casting pearls before swine. Many such ambiguities operate in the novel—to its benefit. Without them it might easily become too simply moralistic, naive in its social commentary and interpretation of human behavior, and frankly pedantic. As it is, Vonnegut manages to reinvigorate the ancient topic of avarice by giving it topicality, by relating it to recent technological developments and their social implications, by showing it specifically as a part of the American class and value systems, and by emphasizing its role in contemporary man's psychosis.

On the other hand, there are defects which weaken this novel. The multiplicity of characters and episodes is less well handled here than in other novels. The early prominence of Mushari, for example, may lead us to wonder what has happened to him as we read on. The Pisquontuit characters are established in some detail, only to sleep their way into obscurity. Episodes like those describing Eliot's fly hunts or Ulm's novel or Selena's life at the orphanage, even if thematically relevant, seem digressive. Eliot himself remains less sharply defined than some of his supporting characters, and his state of mind in the closing scenes which follow his breakdown is uncertainly drawn. Despite the fine comedy, the sharp satire, and the social and moral commentary it contains, *God Bless You, Mr. Rosewater* fails to measure up to the three novels which precede it. It is also more of a traditional "representative" novel than any of them. In his next novel, *Slaughterhouse-Five,* Vonnegut returns to a more venturesome style and we see him again at his best.

VI

The End of the Road:
Slaughterhouse-Five

or The Children's Crusade

In *Slaughterhouse-Five* (1969), Vonnegut comes at last to a direct confrontation with his Dresden experience. He also brings together many of the other things he has talked about in his first five novels. The numerous recapitulations of previous themes, resurrections of characters who have appeared before, and recollections of earlier mentioned incidents in this novel are not just self-parody as they might be in *Cat's Cradle*, nor are they simply the development of a kind of extended in-joke as they might be in the intervening novels. Rather, they represent an attempt at integration, an effort to bring together all that Vonnegut has been saying about the human condition and contemporary American society, and to relate those broad commentaries to the central traumatic, revelatory and symbolic

172

moment of the destruction of Dresden. The event itself, of course, is not the problem. The difficulty lies in trying to say all that the fire-raid means, to one man, to each individual man, to all men collectively. Vonnegut also says the book is a failure. We may not agree; or, if we do, we will probably want to give more credit to the attempt than the author gives himself. The only real failure is that the novel had to be written at all. Whatever its weaknesses (like characterization, a weakness Vonnegut freely admits), the book's achievements are considerable—and more numerous than a first glance suggests. *Slaughterhouse-Five* goes beyond being a therautically autobiographical novel, or simply an anti-war novel, the two categories into which it could be most easily fitted. It is both these things and more—an attempt, in effect, to create a contemporary legend.

Slaughterhouse-Five begins autobiographically with Vonnegut musing about himself—his good friend the dog, late nights drinking, smoking, telephoning long lost friends; teaching at the Writers' Workshop at the University of Iowa—and the fact that he has been telling people for a long time that he was working on a book about the raid on Dresden. He was there during that raid, and its impression has been indelible. He also recalls visiting a veteran friend, "Bernard V. O'Hare," to talk over some of their war experiences. O'Hare's wife, Mary, had appeared hostile, and it emerged that she had feared the book would be a glorification of war, adaptable to a movie starring John Wayne or Frank Sinatra. She had insisted the men were "babies" in the war, and that a glorification would send more children, like theirs upstairs, into more wars. That was when the author agreed to call his story *The Children's Crusade*. With O'Hare he then traveled to Dresden on Guggenheim Fellowship money, looking back like Lot's wife at the ruined city. The book is a failure, he says, because it is written by a pillar of salt.

After this prologue, Vonnegut recounts the story of Billy Pilgrim, focusing upon his capture by the Germans in World War II, his presence in Dresden during the raid, and the consequences of these experiences on his later life. It should be emphasized that the novel does not at all follow the chronological development used in this summary for clarification. Basically there are two major time-streams in the novel; from Billy's becoming lost in Luxembourg in 1944 to his being in Dresden in 1945, and from 1968 to later in the same year. But there are numerous time shifts between these two sequences and to other periods. Seldom do more than two pages fix on one date.

Billy Pilgrim, like his author, was born in 1922. One of his earliest memories is of being taught to swim by his father on the "sink if you don't" system. Other early traumatic experiences occur during a trip West with his family. While he stands tremulously on the brink of the Grand Canyon his mother unexpectedly touches him and he wets his pants. Then he has the life scared out of him when the guide turns out the lights in the Carlsbad Caverns.

After a few unsuccessful weeks in college, Billy goes off to war as a chaplain's assistant. In 1944 the Germans pour into Luxembourg during the Battle of the Bulge, leaving Billy stranded behind enemy lines. He meets up with two scouts and a tank gunner named Roland Weary. For several days this motley foursome searches hopefully for American lines, Billy bobbing up and down on a heel-less shoe. Under the stress of hunger, shock, exhaustion and exposure, Billy loses the will to live and his mind wanders. It is here that he begins to become "unstuck in time"— that is, to find himself living in moments of the past or future. From this point on he frequently knows what will or will not happen to him.

Eventually Billy's slow pace and apparent delirium become too much for the scouts, who depart on their own. This infuriates Weary, who sets about beating up Billy, only being prevented from finishing the job by the arrival of some German irregular soldiers. Weary is forced to give up his shoes in exchange for the feet-cutting hinged clogs of one of the Germans. The two hobbling Americans are herded off to join an ever increasing number of other prisoners being marched into Germany. They are jammed into box cars, which, after sitting in martialling yards for

174

two days, begin a slow journey toward the east. On the ninth day, Weary dies of gangrene from his injured feet. He blames Pilgrim for his plight, and a paranoid little soldier named Paul Lazzaro swears to avenge him by having Billy killed.

Eventually the dilapidated prisoners are unloaded at a camp for Russian POW's, are deloused, showered, given overcoats, and marched into a compound for British officers at the center of the camp. The British POW's are organized, clean, healthy and disciplined, and put on a welcome dinner and pantomime for the new arrivals. The food overwhelms the half-starved Americans, whose unsanitary physical response and general dispiritedness appall the Englishmen. Billy spends a couple of days in the British sickquarters, time-travelling as usual.

Within a few days the Americans march into Dresden to begin work, mainly bottling a honey-like vitamin supplement for pregnant women. They are housed in a slaughterhouse numbered five. At one point they are urged to join the "Free America Corps" to fight the Russians by the American Quisling, Howard Campbell. When the great air raid begins, Campbell, four guards and a hundred of the Americans take shelter in a deep cold storage area. They survive while 135,000 are dying above. When they surface, the ruins of Dresden look like the face of the moon. For a few days the Americans are employed digging in the wreckage. One of them, the earnest former school-teacher Edgar Derby, is executed by a firing squad for taking a teapot from a wrecked building. As the war ends, Billy and his friends are riding around Dresden in a coffin-shaped horse drawn wagon. Billy basks in the sunlight, contentedly time-travelling.

After repatriation, Billy goes to optometrists' school in Ilium. There he meets and marries the college founder's daughter, Valencia. She is a gross, candy-munching woman of limited intellect, but she loves Billy and the two lead a fairly contented life together. They have two children, Barbara and Robert. Robert goes through a period of juvenile delinquency, but emerges as an exemplary Green Beret. Barbara becomes a "bitchy flibbertigibbet" fussing over her father and her husband. Billy thrives as an optometrist, coming eventually to employ five assistants, own shares in other local businesses, earn $60,000 a year, and drive a Cadillac complete with Birch Society bumper stickers supplied by his father-in-law. He continues to time travel, often at moments disconcerting to his patients, so in 1948 he commits himself to a mental hospital. There he shares a ward with Eliot Rosewater, who introduces him to Kilgore Trout's science fiction. Years later, Billy actually meets Kilgore Trout. He discovers the writer ruthlessly supervising a crew of newspaper boys, and invites Trout to his wedding anniversary party.

By 1967, Billy seldom seems to know whether he is here or there—or now or then. On the night of his daughter's wedding he is picked up, as he knows he will be, by a Tralfamadorian flying saucer. Transported to Tralfamadore, he is kept in a luxurious "zoo" where he is mated with a kidnapped movie star, Montana Wildhack. (Billy's absence escapes notice, because by travelling through a time warp his stay of several years on Tralfamadore only means that he is gone from Earth for a microsecond.) The two live almost blissfully, have a child, and then somehow Billy returns. The Tralfamadorians explain Billy's time travelling. To them all times coexist— "whatever is always has been and always will be"—meaning, among other things, that people are always alive at some point in time. They necessarily believe in inevitability and see the conception of free will as a curious Earthling perversion.

In 1968, Billy survives an airplane crash, but with a serious head wound which again hospitalizes him. As the distraught Valencia races to the hospital, she becomes involved in a car accident which rips the exhaust pipes from the Cadillac. On arrival she collapses of carbon monoxide poisoning and dies almost immediately. This time Billy shares his ward with Air Force historian Bertram Copeland Rumfoord, who is writing on the Dresden raid. After his release, Billy visits New York where he goes on a radio talk show to divulge his experiences with

176

the Tralfamadorians. This, and the letters on the same subject he writes to newspapers, convinces his daughter Barbara that he is, at 46, senile.

As Billy sees what happens subsequently, he becomes something of a celebrity, speaking to large crowds about flying saucers, time, and the insignificance of death. On February 13, 1976 (the twenty-first anniversary of the Dresden raid), he is speaking in a stadium in Chicago. (Chicago has been rebuilt, having been hydrogen-bombed by the Chinese. The U.S.A. has been Balkanized into twenty petty nations to end its threat to world peace.) He predicts that he will die within the hour, makes no effort to prevent this, and is shot by a gunman hired by the aged, crazy, but still revengeful Paul Lazarro.

Vonnegut returns to his exterior frame for the story at the end, mentioning the deaths of Senator Robert F. Kennedy, Martin Luther King, his father, and the weekly carnage in Vietnam. He muses that Darwin teaches that "those who die are meant to die, that corpses are improvements" (p. 182). As he and O'Hare fly toward Dresden, he reflects that if the Tralfamadorians are right that we all live forever it does not delight him, but that he is glad to have many happy moments to relive. O'Hare observes that by the year 2,000 the world population will be seven billion. And the author, having given such a bleak portrayal of the individual human's lot on Earth, says sardonically, "I suppose they will all want dignity."

Since the Dresden raid is central to this novel and often mentioned by Vonnegut, here is an historical note. Contrary to some claims, Dresden was *not* an open city, and it did present some targets of military significance. But it had not been bombed before, and the great raid killed few military personnel. At the time, Dresden's population had been doubled by refugees from the East. On the night of February 13/14, about 800 Royal Air Force Lancaster heavy bombers struck in two waves, dropping tons of high explosive bombs and 650,000 incendiaries. The enormous conflagration created was visible 200 miles away. The

177

next day, 450 American B-17 Fortresses dropped more bombs, and P-51 Mustang fighters strafed the wrecked city. Militarily, the raid was immensely successful, very few allied aircraft being shot down while the target was virtually destroyed. Casualties were variously estimated from 35,000 to over 200,000. 135,000, the conservative estimate of the Dresden Police President, is the normally accepted figure. Whether Dresden should have been bombed at all, especially so late in the war, has been questioned. The allies kept details of the raid secret long after.[1]

While *Slaughterhouse-Five* may appear to be wandering and random, an example of Vonnegut's tendencies toward the episodic and the digressive indulged to the extreme, it actually possesses an intricately designed structure. The author's description of his efforts to outline this story, climaxed by his making his "prettiest one" on the back of a roll of wallpaper with his daughter's crayons, seems entirely appropriate. Billy Pilgrim is at one point described as trying to reinvent or restructure his life, while in telling the story Vonnegut tries to give form to the same experiences. At the center of Vonnegut's material—in the wallpaper outline it is cross-hatched across the sheet—is the Dresden raid. From that central event he extends a web outward in time, space and characters. But "web" is a poor metaphor; one might as easily say that he "tunnels into" the experience to find its meaning. Time, space and event coexist and coalesce in this novel, and that is what the structure attempts to convey.

First Vonnegut sets up a frame for the story with the autobiographical prologue in the first chapter. An important preparation for this comes on the title page itself; between the title and a thumbnail biography of the author, Vonnegut describes his book as "A Duty Dance with

---

[1]This summary is drawn from David Irving's *The Destruction of Dresden* (New York: Ballantine Books, 1963)—the work to which Vonnegut refers extensively in *Slaughterhouse-Five*. (Irving's book contains a photograph of a horse-drawn wagon on which Pilgrim's "coffin shaped wagon" could be based.)

Death." The autobiographical first chapter is matched by a return to more of the same in the last chapter, completing the frame, but in such a way as to integrate the frame with the main narrative. The framing device and the interrelationship of the autobiographical with the narrative are strengthened by periodic intrusions by the author throughout the novel: "I was there" or "that was me" (see pp. 58, 109, 129, 140.) "A Dance" is an apt description for the interwoven pattern of the narrative, with the author himself occasionally appearing as one of the dancers. All of the events portrayed are carefully interconnected, and events from "separate" times are often juxtaposed, completing or commenting upon one another. The frequent complementary nature of the time fragments adds to their coherence, although there is surprisingly little difficulty in following this seemingly disjointed narrative. The prologue to the first chapter, and the quick general guidelines to Billy's life in the second, provide the reader with a strong sense of direction from the outset.

The title page gives another clue to the structure of *Slaughterhouse-Five*: "This is a novel somewhat in the telegraphic schizophrenic manner of tales of the planet Tralfamadore, where the flying saucers come from." It might seem absurd to take such an obviously spoofing account at all seriously. The description of the Tralfamadorian novel represents characteristic Vonnegutian self-derision, like the portraits of Kilgore Trout, but as parody it makes some real sense. The Tralfamadorian novel is made up of "clumps of symbols" each of which " 'is a brief, urgent message—describing a situation, a scene.' " Tralfamadorians read these simultaneously, not consecutively. " 'There isn't any particular relationship between all the messages, except that the author has chosen them carefully, so that, when seen all at once, they produce an image of life that is beautiful and inspiring and deep' " (p. 76). Aside from the fact that the Tralfamadorians, in their novels as in their minds, emphasize beautiful moments and exclude the unpleasant ones, *Slaughterhouse-Five* almost fits their requirements. Most of the situations described are grim, many downright painful.

179

The "clumps of symbols" obviously cannot be read simultaneously, either, but the way in which short scenes from several points in time are spliced together does help sustain the impression of concurrent actions, and intensifies the sense of an interrelationship of events transcending time. Nor is there always a "particular relationship between all the messages," but they often do show a kinship of theme or image, and they cohere to create "an image of life" which, while not always "beautiful," is frequently "surprising" and in total effect quite "deep." Because all of its scenes cannot be read simultaneously, the book comes closer to possessing a climax than does the Tralfamadorian novel. It is hard to single out one climactic event, be it the raid itself or the ironic execution of Edgar Derby, but the novel certainly builds toward the end where the meaning, the questions and the emotional impact come together.

In order that this discussion itself avoid the "telegraphic schizophrenic manner," it might be well to pay attention first to the nucleus of the novel, namely Billy Pilgrim and his experiences during the war, in the Dresden raid, and on his trip to Tralfamadore. As already mentioned, there are limitations to the characterization of Billy; limitations which seem to go beyond those explained by Vonnegut at one point in the novel. "There are almost no characters in this story," he says, "and almost no dramatic confrontations, because most of the people in it are so sick and so much the listless playthings of enormous forces. One of the main effects of war, after all, is that people are discouraged from being characters" (pp. 140-141). Some of that we can accept, but some we may question. Vonnegut makes the point here that Edgar Derby is about to act as a character. Others, like the British officers, Weary, and even Paul Lazzaro, become "characters" as opposed to "listless playthings" apparently *because* of this confrontation with war situations. The circumstances imposed do seem to lessen the possibilities of "dramatic confrontations," most of the characters *are* sick, and many of them are manipulated by "enormous forces" in ways which limit their freedom for character defining actions.

Furthermore, the whole design of the novel calls for much of the cast to make only brief appearances which, while they might create striking impressions, are not of the sort to develop characterizations. Yet most of these observations do not really apply to the protagonist.

Billy Pilgrim is both sick and a listless plaything, but that part of his characterization works quite well. His physical ailments and his vulnerability to controlling forces are even more extensive than those of Eliot Rosewater in *God Bless You, Mr. Rosewater*, and impose some of the same burdens on characterization, yet in this respect Billy seems at least as convincing as Eliot. The ambiguities of his sanity or insanity are more extreme than those surrounding Eliot. They represent the culmination of a progression which begins with Paul Proteus' moral uncertainty, which becomes psychologically more complex in the uncertain truths of Howard Campbell's self-analyses, and which incorporates questions of morality, motivations and sanity in the case of Eliot Rosewater. The very uncertainties and ambiguities of Billy Pilgrim as shocked, uncomprehending and listless victim add conviction to his characterization in that role. Billy grinning foolishly at Germans who abuse him, Billy in a delirium of fatigue in the boxcar, even Billy weeping silently years after the war, emerges as touchingly lifelike. In other roles he does not.

Perhaps the problem arises from the number of roles Billy must fulfill. The novel concerns itself not just with Dresden or the war, but with a much broader depiction of a human condition which these events emblematize. At the center of such a work, Billy becomes, as his name distinctly suggests, a contemporary pilgrim progressing through an absurd world—except that he does not really progress. Being an Everyman proves tricky in the age of specialization. Billy must be innocent Adam falling into the terrible wisdom of the twentieth century. He portrays a modern version of the Christ figure more than once. He is the child duped into the children's crusade. He becomes a credulous and adaptable Gulliver on a voyage to another world. And he is asked to fulfill the roles of prosperous

businessman, polished convention speaker, crank partici-
pant in talk shows, and death-denigrating messiah of
quasi-religious crusades. Understandably, his characterization proves unequal to all these roles. Eliot Rosewater's
recovery from shell shock to become successful foundation administrator seems plausible enough; it simply marks
a return to his established life style. His becoming bene-
factor to the poor similarly has adequate motivation. It
proves much more difficult to reconcile the predominant
image of Billy the bemused POW with the $60,000-a-year
optometrist-businessman, even given that he married the
boss's daughter. Vonnegut asks us to give him that—and
to laboriously document Billy's ascending career would
indeed be irrelevant to the novel's purposes. We might
ask *why* Billy must become a $60,000-a-year optometrist,
unless it is to emphasize the helpless child at the mercy
of indomitable forces within the controlling businessman.
Or unless, of course, the $60,000-a-year optometrist *is*
the modern Everyman. We do know that Billy weeping
silently, dozing off into time travel, blundering embar-
rassedly in a porno bookstore, or jiggling on his electronic
bed fits consistently with the shattered soldier, and that
it is hard to see how a chap like that could successfully
run even a shoeshine stand. Shell-shocked veterans have
made competent businessmen. Henry Green shows how
in *Back,* and Vonnegut makes it plausible with Eliot
Rosewater, but the chamber of commerce side of Billy
Pilgrim never comes alive.

At the core of the characterization of Billy Pilgrim is
the conception of war as a children's crusade. The starting
point for this analogy is Mary O'Hare's insistence that
men like to give war an aura of glamor as a mature mas-
culine activity whereas in fact it is fought by mere babies.
The author concurs—"We *had* been foolish virgins in the
war, right at the end of childhood' " (p. 13). And his
promise to call the book "The Children's Crusade" leads
him and Bernard O'Hare to look up some facts about
the title event. They discover that the Children's Crusade
began in 1213, the idea of two monks who planned to
assemble an army of children and sell them as slaves in

182

North Africa. Accordingly, 30,000 volunteer children were marched to Marseilles, half subsequently being drowned in shipwrecks and half indeed being sold into slavery. A few went to Genoa, where there were no ships waiting, and were treated kindly by the local people. The obvious parallels with the raising of a modern army are that the people sent to die are in both cases young, innocent, and uncomprehending, that the patriotic fervor of onlookers and influential persons urges on both enterprises, that too many die needlessly while too few are treated humanely, and that the declared "noble" intentions may bear little relation to the actual purposes or accomplishments of the enterprise. In each case, mere children find themselves the hapless pawns of forces they neither understand nor can resist. Young of face, gawky of stature and childishly perplexed, Billy Pilgrim, who like the crusader starts out on a holy mission as chaplain's assistant, makes the perfect representational figure for this conception of war.

The affinity between men at war and children emerges in several ways. Among the most obvious is the youth of Billy himself and of other soldiers. Two German troopers, in particular, are merely boys in their teens. The colonel who commands the British prisoners makes the point explicit, saying that having been prisoners since the beginning of hostilities, his group had imagined the war being fought by men of their age. After he sees the Americans shaved and cleaned, he realizes for the first time how young they are and is shocked. " ' "My God, my God—" ' I said to myself, ' "it's the Children's Crusade" ' " (p. 91). Vonnegut underlines the resemblance more than once, as when he qualifies his description of "Wild Bob's" regiment as about forty-five hundred men by saying "—a lot of children, actually" (p. 57). The character of "Wild Bob" helps make another observation on children at war: that men at war become as children in fact if they are not in age. This colonel from Wyoming has always wanted his men to call him "Wild Bob" (they never have), as if he boyishly envisions himself fulfilling the role of a military "character," hero and friend to his troops—whom he has in fact led to disaster. Similarly, Roland Weary wistfully envisions himself as one of "the Three Musketeers," and dreams romantically of valor and loyalty. The two scouts will not play his game. Fittingly, the entertainment the Englishmen provide for the Americans is a modified children's pantomime, and when the British recoil from their "guests" they divide the camp compound by the old childhood technique of scraping a groove in the ground with the heel. These and similar instances emphasize the childlike nature of men at war not so much to say that war is childish as to indicate the haplessness of men caught up in war, like children somehow swept up in an adult barroom brawl. They also suggest that men made helpless, shocked, dazed, bullied and maimed in war are driven back into themselves in regressive ways. War *might* be childish in some ways—the referees of the American war games arguing over who is "dead," or the Germans "capturing" for the cameras the already captive Billy could be taken to suggest this—but that is not the main thrust of Vonnegut's anti-war theme. He seems most concerned to show war as a terrifying unleashing of monstrous forces which sweeps up the innocent children of men to destroy and enslave them.

That particular emphasis to Vonnegut's war-criticism, and beyond that to his diagnosis of the contemporary human condition, necessitates that he extend—even mythicize—his presentation of Billy Pilgrim as universal man-child. The name begins the job, and the allusions to Jesus Christ and Adam continue it. One of Trout's novels, *The Gospel from Outer Space,* sets the tone and the direction of the Christ references. Trout's spaceman, having studied Christianity, finds it hard to understand how Christians can so easily be cruel. He concludes that whereas the Gospels *mean* to teach mercy to even the lowest of things, they actually taught this: "*Before you kill somebody, make absolutely sure he isn't well connected*" (p. 94). Consequently the modern reader of the Gospels comes to the story of men killing the Son of God and thinks that the killers made a mistake, as if killing Jesus had he *not* been the Son of God would have been all right. The spaceman's gospel has God take a different line: *"From this moment on, He will punish horribly anybody who torments a bum who has no connections!"* (p. 95). Soldier Billy, if not Businessman Billy, fills the role of bum-Jesus admirably, and makes an excellent vehicle for the demonstration of those morals about showing mercy to even the lowest.

Other Christ allusions show Billy wandering in a wilderness, being falsely accused and made a scapegoat (by Weary, who blames Pilgrim for his death), being reviled by the other inmates of the boxcar, and hanging from a crossbar in one corner, "self-crucified" (p. 69). Later, as he lies dozing in the cart after the Dresden raid, he hears voices which sound to him like "the tones . . . used by the friends of Jesus when they took His ruined body down from His cross" (p. 169). Ironically, those tones are not meant for him but for the pathetic horses drawing the cart. Billy cries for those horses, and weeps often later, always silently. Vonnegut observes that "in *that* respect, at least, he resembled the Christ of the carol: *The cattle are lowing,/ The Baby awakes./ But the little Lord Jesus/ No crying He makes*" (p. 170). (That carol also provides the novel's epigraph.) Vonnegut's saying "in *that* respect, at least," implies his rather self-consciously putting a qualification on the Christ role of Billy, but that he definitely does intend Billy to be viewed thus in *at least that* one respect. The identification can be taken seriously if not solemnly. At times it becomes ludicrous—but that is exactly the point. Billy's being moonishly bemused, utterly helpless, even ridiculous, fits him for the role of persecuted child, of babe born to die.

Perhaps the most important allusion to Adam comes at the time of Billy's capture. The German corporal wears a pair of golden cavalry boots taken from a Hungarian colonel. As he waxes them, he tells recruits, " 'If you look in there deep enough, you'll see Adam and Eve' " Obviously the only way that could happen would be for a recruit to see the Adam and Eve within himself, which is essentially what Billy does when he sees the naked couple within the boots' lustre. "They were so innocent, so vulnerable, so eager to behave decently. Billy Pilgrim loved them" (p. 46). Innocent, vulnerable, eager to please—the description applies aptly to Billy. When the fifteen year old German soldier is labelled "as beautiful as Eve," the association of Billy with Adam becomes even stronger. This allusion, like those to Christ, has its comic under-cutting. The nearest Billy comes to being Adam in a literal sense might be when he and Montana Wildhack live naked in the geodesic paradise of the Tralfamadorian zoo. But while these identifications are made almost laughingly, as the tone of the novel demands, they are explicit. They extend the dimensions and significance of Billy's role, con-tributing to the expansion of the book to a more universal scope than that of anti-war novel alone.

The character of Billy gives *Slaughterhouse-Five* a point of focus, particularly for the emotions generated by the wide ranging action of the story. In that respect, this novel proves more successful than *Cat's Cradle* which in several ways resembles *Slaughterhouse-Five* more closely than do the other four novels. (*Cat's Cradle* also speaks of the Children's Crusade, of mass destruction, war and the moral questions they generate, uses numerous references to other works by Vonnegut, and spreads itself over a similar wide range of times, episodes, and social issues.) The war, and Dresden in particular, also gives focus, in a way which again invites contrast to *Cat's Cradle*. The narrative device used in that novel is that Jonah has been trying to write about "the day the world ended"—the day Hiroshima was bombed—but has been unable to do so. He does ultimately write about the day the world ends, but the final catastrophe by *ice-nine*, while giving tone to the narrative and providing the context for the considera-tions of ethics, religion, politics and art, does not become a dominating event in itself. The Dresden raid does achieve such centrality in *Slaughterhouse-Five*. Everything that happens points forward or backward to Dresden. If the war becomes the general metaphor for Vonnegut's vision of the human condition, Dresden becomes the symbol, the quintessence. It acts as something concrete, a specific point of reference, to which all that is said about human behavior or the nature of man's existence can be related. For example, who better fitted to ask that recurring question "Why me?" than the victims—or the survivors—of Dresden? Or what better example of the absurd than this, the Allies' most "successful" application of bombing in the European theater, being directed at a non-target? The Dresden raid, together with the character of Billy Pilgrim, helps unify and focus the disparate elements of the novel. As an actual event realistically portrayed, the raid adds intensity to the questions, denunciations, and pathos in the novel, as compared to that generated by fictional disasters in the earlier books. That fact also greatly affects the tone of the novel, making it more serious, more terrifying and more moving than *Cat's Cradle*.

The moral and psychological context for the depiction of the Dresden raid is set up in the first chapter. There we see essentially two perspectives; the highly personal recollections of the author who was involved in the event, and the detached, distant view of history. The latter is introduced in the account of the destruction of Sodom and Gomorrah which the author reads in his motel Gideon Bible. It suggests that "Those were vile people in both those cities, as is well known. The world was better off without them" (p. 19). Obviously, he does not share that harsh moral view, and his sympathies lie with Lot's wife who looks back to where people and homes had been— an act he finds lovable because it is so human. The Biblical account provides a precedent for Dresden; a city destroyed in righteous wrath, people judged evil and ripe for annihilation, and an observer who looks back wonderingly, touched by human compassion. Some of the parallel moral questions posed by such great destructions are obvious. So the people of Sodom and Gomorrah were a bad lot— does that justify their obliteration? So the Germans had devastated Warsaw, Rotterdam, Coventry and East London, and had sent millions to their deaths in other ways— does that make moral the destruction of Dresden? Vonnegut makes considerable effort to incorporate official and historical assessments of such raids into his novel by quoting from President Truman's announcement of the atom-bombing of Hiroshima and from David Irving's book, *The Destruction of Dresden.* The Truman statement, made in time of war, essentially argues that the destruction of Hiroshima was necessary to save civilization from the destruction wreaked by the Japanese. The two forwards to Irving's book, written by Lieutenant General Ira C. Eaker, U.S.A.F., and Air Marshal Sir Robert Saundby, R.A.F., some time after the war, struggle with the moral issues, regretting so many deaths in a militarily unnecessary raid but insisting that they be viewed in the context of the even more massive slaughters wrought by the Germans.

Vonnegut's comment on these official assessments comes in the rambling words of Billy Pilgrim: " 'If you're ever in Cody, Wyoming . . . just ask for Wild Bob' " (p. 162). Wild Bob was the colonel who had led his troops to disaster, lost his regiment, then tried to assure his soldiers they had "nothing to be ashamed of" because they had left a lot of Germans dead, too (p. 58). Yet Wild Bob remains a sympathetic character. Perhaps through him Vonnegut observes that military men responsible for such slaughters act not out of malignity but from muddled values which prevent them from seeing simpler moral truths. Treated less sympathetically than the commander who makes a mistake is the military historian who later tries to justify the error. Illustrating this role is Bertram Copeland Rumfoord, "the official Air Force historian," writing his one volume history of the U.S.A.A.F. in World War II. He feels obliged to mention Dresden because so many people now know that it was worse than Hiroshima. The raid has been cloaked in secrecy for years lest it be criticized by "a lot of bleeding hearts," Rumfoord says, and he seems bent only on dismissing any notion that it might be a blemish on the glorious record of the Air Force. So intent is he on treating Dresden with official "detachment" that he shuts out any possible firsthand reports from Billy Pilgrim. He seems only concerned to convince Billy, as his readers, that "it *had* to be done"— while remaining rather uneasy himself.

Posed against the official assessments are episodes involving two lesser characters which serve to expose Dresden to a different moral viewpoint. The Sodom and Gomorrah reference, the allusion to Hiroshima and the historical judgments on Dresden all involve looking at the raid from a distance, taking an overview of it, placing it in a large historical context. The stories of Paul Lazarro and Edgar Derby, like those of Lot's wife and Billy Pilgrim, reverse the perspective, measuring the larger event against individual human consequences. Paul Lazarro typifies those miserable little men, inviting our pity as much as our disgust, who are as close as Vonnegut ever gets to creating villains. He threatens to have Billy killed, and actually does have him killed years later. In the prison camp he tries to steal an English officer's watch, gets caught in the act, and suffers a severe mauling. Characteristically, he swears he will have the Englishman killed—a stranger will knock at his door, announce he comes from Paul Lazarro, "shoot his pecker off," give him a couple of minutes to think about that, then kill him. He also tells a tender story of how he once fed a dog steak containing sharpened fragments of clocksprings. This twisted little crank feeds on revenge—"the sweetest thing in life"—yet he takes no satisfaction from the destruction of Dresden. He bears the Germans no grudge, and he prides himself on never harming an innocent bystander (pp. 119-121). The obvious moral object lesson here is that in some ways even a sordid monster like Lazarro can be superior to the saviors of civilization, who also take revenge, who kill those who have done them no harm in ways every bit as horrible as anything the warped mind of Lazarro could conceive and with no thought for innocent bystanders. The second incident involves Edgar Derby, who is arrested and shot by the Germans for plundering when caught with a perfectly ordinary teapot taken from a ruined house. This time we observe the irony of a society which condones massive destruction but which executes a man—one who tries bravely to be decent and moral—for salvaging a teapot from that wreckage.

These two minor incidents give scale to the inhumanity and moral dubiousness of the Dresden raid. The disaster itself remains so massive as to be hard to register in any other way. Statistics of the numbers killed and the houses destroyed, or descriptions of the ruins lying like the surface of the moon, remain too large, too general, too abstract. Particular images like human bodies reduced to charred logs or girls boiled alive in a water tower, and personal episodes like those involving Lazarro and Derby, stick in the mind. The same is true for Billy. The horror of the total nightmare registers in the little things, like the four distraught German guards, huddled together, mouths open but not knowing what to say, looking like a barber-shop quartet singing (and here the irony borders on excess) "That Old Gang of Mine." " 'So long forever,' old sweethearts and pals—God bless 'em—' " (p. 153). And after all that he has suffered and the carnage he has witnessed among the debris, it takes the sight of those wretched horses drawing his cart to reduce Billy to tears.

The significance of the Dresden firestorm, then, is weighed on the scale of time, from Sodom and Gomorrah down to Hiroshima, and on the scale of human response, from the collective, public view of the official history to the personal nightmare of Billy Pilgrim. It is also measured spatially, in effect, through the perspective afforded by the use of science fiction. Billy tells the Tralfamadorians about wars on Earth, and what a great threat to all life the inhabitants of his planet must be. The Tralfamadorians regard his concerns as stupid. They know how the Universe ends, and Earth has nothing to do with it. Their own experiments with flying-saucer fuels end the Universe. In any case, they tell Billy, Tralfamadore is not as peaceful as he seems to think. They have wars as dreadful as anything Billy knows about. Once again the point of view of a more sophisticated being from another planet provides commentary on human behavior, yet this time it might surprise us as much as it does Billy. The Tralfamadorians' timeless view is not that Earthlings are senseless and barbaric to engage in war, a menace to themselves and the Universe. It is that Billy is ridiculous to expect such a logical projection of the future to work in an absurd Universe, and that he exaggerates the importance of the human role in the cosmos. In particular, he over-emphasizes free will and fails to recognize that the tragedies of war and ultimate destruction occur, like all things, because that is the way the moment is structured. They advocate acceptance of life's cruelties and catastrophes, saying "so it goes" to each, then turning their thoughts to happier things.

That position has a certain undeniable logic, especially to beings capable of time-travel. For one thing, it avoids putting them constantly at odds with the essential nature of an Absurd Universe. For another, it makes sense given their conception of time, where past, present and future are all fixed and determinate. Whatever will be, is; whatever has been, is; whatever is, always has been and always will be. We need not accept the Tralfamadorian view of life to recognize that it represents a commentary on the human lot. For the events of the novel point to a world in which things happen which are beyond our control, in which what we try to control even with the best of intentions often goes awry, and where the forces which shape our destinies are beyond our comprehension even if they are more than simply "the structure of the moment." If the circumstances of existence are thus, then the motto which we are shown once hanging on Billy's wall and once hanging between Montana Wildhack's breasts—"God grant me the serenity to accept the things I cannot change, courage to change the things I can, and wisdom always to tell the difference" (pp. 52, 181)— proves ironic to say the least. As the narrator comments: "Among the things Billy Pilgrim could not change were the past, the present, and the future" (p. 52). Or, in other words, accept everything with serenity. Thus the lesson of Tralfamadore has much in common with the admonition to Lot's wife not to look back to Sodom and with Rumfoord's attitude of leaving the history of the Dresden raid as nearly forgotten as possible. It is also implicit in Vonnegut's saying that his book remains a failure because it

191

was written by someone who, like Lot's wife, had been turned into a pillar of salt.

But Kurt Vonnegut looks back. Here the structure of the novel becomes vital to its meaning, for Vonnegut not only looks back to his own Dresden experience but to his previous fiction. If the earlier novels have all been pointing toward Dresden, he now draws arrows back to them, as it were, to connect them with the climactic event. Tracing all of these echoes and repetitions, showing how they unite to produce a cumulative depiction of a world and a pattern of existence emblematized in Dresden and its impact on Billy Pilgrim, would be tedious. The method and effect of the device can be illustrated with a selection of recurrent images, themes, characters or simple incidents.

In the first place, it should be recognized that Billy Pilgrim represents the culmination of a number of traits present in a progressively increasing degree in the earlier protagonists. *Cat's Cradle* makes such generalizations about Vonnegut's protagonists difficult, because its narrator remains something of a non-protagonist. Making allowance for exceptions in that case, however, it becomes possible to deduce some patterns. Each of the protagonists is at least partially a victim of circumstances, either social or cosmic, which effectively control his destiny. The protagonists of the first three novels become captives in a literal way, Jonah and Eliot both undergo confinements, and Billy becomes the prisoner of Germans and Tralfamadorians. Each endures a scene of desolation, from the wrecking of Ilium to the Martian war on Earth to Eliot's imagined firestorm in Indianapolis, leading up to the Dresden conflagration. Faced with the terrors of an absurd, uncontrollable and frequently hostile environment, each is driven toward some form of evasion. As if reality becomes too much to bear, each moves into some kind of unreality or seeming unreality. Emotional disturbance, neurosis, and possible madness emerge in a developing pattern, from Proteus' momentary suspicions of his own mental health to Billy's having himself committed. At least at some point in their lives, all are financially successful men, yet prosperity has little correlation with peace of mind, as the silently weeping optometrist-businessman Billy demonstrates. Most of them have ambivalent feelings toward their fathers which *might* have something to do with their social views but more probably do not. As the prosecutor suggests Proteus' actions express resentment of his father, so Pilgrim's psychiatrist thinks the scares his father has biven Billy cause his condition. Both judgments ignore the obvious motivations. But the gulf between father and child parallels that between controlling forces and the man. All follow a literal journey which accompanies the psychological voyage toward awareness. Each is reviled by a society whose moral values are inferior to those it judges warped in the protagonist. Yet each struggles with morality, tries to be a moral man, and evinces an enduring concern to give purpose and goodness to life.

The essential pattern emerges of an unheroic man who is wanderer and prisoner in an absurd universe, a perpetual child dominated by forces he scarce understands, shocked and stunned by incomprehensible horrors, yet somehow finding happiness in moments of joy and love, and doggedly persisting in the effort to be a decent person and to find meaning in existence. Billy epitomizes most of these characteristics. His story may not as fully demonstrate every phase of the pattern as does that of Malachi Constant, but through the war scenes and the central event of Dresden it generates a peculiar force. Dresden becomes the one metaphor around which *Slaughterhouse-Five* builds, like a poem probing the arrested moment and its implications with vivid intensity. (In that respect it might be seen as roughtly akin to a poem like Yeat's "Leda and the Swan," building outward or—again the ambiguity—delving inward from its climactic symbolic event, the rape of Leda by Zeus, to the Trojan war and speculations beyond.) By comparison, *The Sirens of Titan* remains more purely narrative in form, demonstrating and explaining its thesis. Billy Pilgrim, wanderer and prisoner on Earth and in space alike, Jesus and Adam, optometrist-businessman and modest loving husband, talk-show crank and preacher of life-in-spite-of-death, traumatized survivor of Dresden, brings together the elements of the pattern in a version of twentieth century combination saint and everyman.

From *Player Piano* comes the setting for the American scenes of *Slaughterhouse-Five*: Ilium, New York. The industrial giant located in Ilium varies from novel to novel, but it remains essentially a one company town. The successive Iliums with their particular resident industries represent the way so many American cities are in fact dominated by one industry or one group of industries— Seattle by Boeing, Detroit by auto manufacturers. But the device goes much further than this, Ilium becoming a representative unit of the larger industrial society, a demonstration-piece for aspects of life under American capitalism. The characteristics developed to an extreme in *Player Piano* recur: domination by a new technological-managerial elite, working masses either being replaced by automation or rendered automatons themselves, people without sense of purpose or self esteem. In Billy's Ilium, the ghetto residents have felt such futility that they have burned down their own neighborhood, making it look like Dresden after being fire-bombed (p. 51). Nothing could make more explicit the resemblance between what man is doing to man in Ilium and what man did to man in Dresden. Another echo from *Player Piano* comes in images of loneliness, surely an appropriate emotion in the inhabitants of such an environment. One of these images, which occurs several times in Vonnegut's work and twice in *Slaughterhouse-Five,* is of a big dog barking somewhere far off. Each time the sound is the same: "With the help of fear and echoes and winter silences, that dog had a voice like a big bronze gong" (pp. 42, 71). We might recall Winston Niles Rumfoord's terrible isolation in being sent finally into endless space without even his dog, Kazak, or the gong-like bark seeming to portend his fate which Constant hears as he enters Rumfoord's estate. Billy hears the gong-bark as he wanders in Luxembourg and as he enters the prison camp—it acts as a signal emphasizing the loneliness of his dual fate as wanderer-prisoner.

From *The Sirens of Titan,* by way of later appearances,

194

come the Rumfoords. Some of the attributes ascribed to this selectively-bred stock in *The Sirens of Titan* seem both admirable and sincerely intended by Vonnegut. On the other hand, they are typically aloof, somewhat out of touch, lacking in human warmth and compassion. The honeymooning Pilgrims cannot fail to be aware of the passing yacht *Scheherazade*, but on board the honeymooning Lance Rumfoords are a thousand and one nights away from the Pilgrims or anyone like them. The capacities which the Rumfoords have nurtured, which have brought them to power and wealth, are the same ones which allow Bertram Rumfoord to treat both Billy and the story of Dresden so dispassionately or Winston Rumfoord to use people for his own ends with the assurance that his machinations were for their own good. Bertram's insistance that Billy has echolalia demonstrates such attitudes: "Rumfoord was thinking in a military manner: that an inconvenient person, one whose death he wished for very much, for practical reasons, was suffering from a repulsive disease" (p. 166). It is easy to see how he can conclude that Dresden "*had* to be done," and how the Rumfoord approach, subjugating means to ends, individuals to programs, conscience to ambition, will always lead to Dresdens.

Tralfamadore, space and time travel, and visions of a fixed future which negates free will also come from *The Sirens of Titan*. The science fiction element in *Slaughterhouse-Five* shares the basic ingredients it provides in other novels: an outside perspective on human affairs; a means of projecting the mundane to bizarre extremes which expose its characteristics by exaggeration; a literal "universalizing" of given conditions. Billy's journey to Tralfamadore and his being placed in a zoo there act in part as parallels to his wanderings in Luxembourg and his internment in the German camp, emphasizing that the war experiences are not unique ones dependent upon particular circumstances but are emblematic of the general condition of man in the cosmos. The Tralfamadorian insistence that things happen simply becaue that is "the way the moment was structured" and that people in time are like insects

195

trapped in a blob of amber also emphasizes the condition of man in broad existential terms. The space story provides a context for the war episodes. Picked up by the Tralfamadorians, Billy's only question is, "Why me?" (p. 66). His captors explain that there is no *why*—it just is. Soon afterwards, in the counterpointed narrative of the German prisoners, an American is unexpectedly struck by a guard. "Why me?" he asks. " 'Vy you? Vy anybody?' " responds the guard (p. 79). In short, the story of Billy's capture and of Dresden, with its insistent *whys* and its persistent absurd inevitability provides the perfect embodiment of the vision of existence which the Tralfamadorian episodes in Vonnegut diagram.

There is another aspect of the science fiction, also pervasive in *The Sirens of Titan*, which calls attention to itself in *Slaughterhouse-Five*. That is the element of evasion or escape. For while the science fiction stresses grim aspects of existence—inevitability, meaninglessness, alienation and isolation, the absurd—it remains itself an escape into imagination and fancy. This ambivalence of science fiction contributes to the mixed tone common in Vonnegut, strongest in *The Sirens of Titan* but considerable in this novel, of cutting satirical exposure balanced by wistful expression of tenderness, of harsh visions of the existential void mingled with lingering glimpses of a warmer world. At the same time that Billy's space journey extends the existential terms of his earthly journey, it also contains some of the happiest, most comforting moments of his life. The Tralfamadorians themselves seem kind, and apparently do their best to treat Billy with understanding. He feels as happy there as on earth, his little zoo world seems cozy, and his relationship with Montana Wildhack is a loving one. In fact, it looks almost like erotic dream come true combined with ideal matrimonial harmony, the sweet innocence of Adam and Eve re-created in the snug safety of a geodesic Eden. And while the Tralfamadorians confirm his experience of inevitable subjection to incomprehensible forces, they also provide him with an answer. The perpetual existence of all moments of time removes the negation of death. As surely as man dies man is always alive in those moments that he lived. That is the vision that Billy preaches in the final years of his life and which enables him to face the death he has foreseen without fear or regret.

If in these respects the time and space travel looks like wish-fulfillment or escape from reality, that is entirely appropriate. We must surely wonder, like his daughter and others in the novel, if all Billy's talk of Tralfamadore and time travel is not madness. When Billy commits himself he shares his room with Eliot Rosewater. Eliot has killed a fourteen-year-old German fireman and Billy has seen "the greatest massacre in European history," and both find life meaningless. "So they were trying to re-invent themselves and their universe. Science fiction was a big help" (p. 87). That comment could suggest that all the time and space travels are tricks of Billy's mind, "oubliettes" into which it escapes as the only way to make life bearable. The first time Billy "flips out" he is exhausted, cold, hungry, scared and in pain: hallucinatory escape from reality in such circumstances seems completely plausible. Subsequently there are interconnections between "reality" and the time travel which help suggest the latter could be dreams or hallucinations derived from the former. The idea of a man and woman being kidnapped by space men and displayed in a zoo occurs in a Kilgore Trout novel Billy reads (p. 174). Orange and black stripes appear on the locomotive of the POW train, on the tent used for daughter Barbara's wedding reception, and on the moonlit hall wall as Billy walks to the flying saucer (p. 62). Some room remains for lingering suspicions that all the science fiction elements exist only in Billy's mind (as the Indianapolis conflagration exists only in Eliot's mind in *God Bless You, Mr. Rosewater*), even though the story is told as if they were factual. That would not diminish their impact or their service to theme, and it would even intensify the poignancy of the sufferings inflicted on Billy by his experience. Nor does the possible ambiguity weaken the story. As with the moral uncertainties surrounding Campbell's confessions in *Mother Night*, we have it both ways, in effect, so that the range of psychological and thematic exploration is broadened.

The science fiction technique, then, dramatizes the general condition of man in an Absurd Universe captured metaphorically and literally in the Dresden episode, and expresses the inevitable desire to escape at least momentarily from such a vision of reality. *Mother Night* showed the same wartime nightmare and the same wish for evasion. The connection with that novel comes partly through the general images of human suffering in wartime, partly through the similar depiction of the rights and wrongs of both sides in the war, and through the character of Howard Campbell. In most respects, the Campbell of *Slaughterhouse-Five* seems consistent with the one seen in *Mother Night*, though curiously one detail does not fit—this time he is married to *Resi* Noth, not Helga. Another detail carried over from the same novel is the "Blue Fairy Godmother." In *Mother Night* that was Campbell's name for the American intelligence officer who recruited him. This time it is the appellation for a British prisoner, deriving from the role he plays in the welcoming pantomime. Campbell's main function consists of commenting on the nature of American prisoners in general, tracing their behavior to the influence of their native class system. That system is described in terms resembling those declared in *God Bless You, Mr. Rosewater*. The American enlisted men, Campbell says, despise themselves because they see their poverty as a sign of their own failure. They love neither themselves nor one another, reject any leadership from among their ranks as pretension by someone no better than they are, and therefore make sulky, self-pitying prisoners (pp. 111-113). If the portrayal of men as prisoners of war is seen as a metaphor for the general condition of man, then the consequences of the system decried in *God Bless You, Mr. Rosewater* are shown in *Slaughterhouse-Five* not just for what they do to Americans as soldiers and prisoners but for their larger human cost.

Other repetitions abound. Those references to writing about days of catastrophe and to the Children's Crusade from *Cat's Cradle* have already been mentioned. As in that book, there is talk here of fabrication being necessary to explain life, when Eliot Rosewater tells a psychiatrist, " 'I think you guys are going to have to come up with a lot of wonderful *new* lies, or people just aren't going to want to go on living' " (pp. 87-88). The frightening incomprehensibility which demands lies in *Cat's Cradle* is intensified in the senseless horror of Dresden. Well might the questioning bird call, surely an existential "Why?" which punctuates other novels as it does this one, provide the last word—"*Poo-tee-weet?*"

In sum, the allusions to other novels serve to enlarge and complete the significance of the central action of *Slaughterhouse-Five*, while this novel in turn draws together what has been shown in the earlier ones. It also gathers the multiple episodes of its own story into its main symbolic event. All the contemporary events depicted— ghetto riot, Vietnam war, assassinations of Martin Luther King and Robert F. Kennedy—become part of the existential absurdity crystallized in the firebombing of Dresden. Everything is united in a consistent, concise vision of the world according to Vonnegut. That vision remains descriptive more than interpretive, but the carefully assembled events speak vividly and the moral imperatives emerge with force. The structural technique employed in *Slaughterhouse-Five* gives a short novel depth, complexity and inclusiveness, all delivered with an impact intensified by compression.

Having shown us the hideous reality and the universal ramifications of the destruction of Dresden, what does Vonnegut offer us with which to meet such a world? On the face of it, very little. The general implications of this story might be that war and hate and various forms of cruelty are bad. There is nothing new in that, although the force with which these stock observations are made does revitalize their horror and perhaps reinvigorate our conviction that such things must cease. As the movie producer says to the author on hearing he has written an anti-war novel, " 'Why don't you write an anti-*glacier* book instead?' " (p. 3). Perhaps Vonnegut accepts the challenge in extending *Slaughterhouse-Five* into more than an anti-war novel. The pens of anti-war writers may never be mightier than swords, and the voices of men crying out against the absurdity of existence may echo away in the recesses of unheeding space, but there is morality and humanity in man's making the effort. As Vonnegut says of Lot's wife, he loves her for looking back because it was such a human thing to do. Vonnegut looks back, and the result is a very human book. Both of them, he says, are turned into pillars of salt. The implication seems to be that to look back at such a catastrophe, at so much human suffering, is to become immobilized by sorrow, to be so caught up in the horror and grief of what life has brought as to be unable to go on living. That might be what is meant by Billy Pilgrim's becoming "unstuck in time." Shocked by his experience, trapped in the memory of horrors, he cannot go on living moment by consecutive moment. At this point the quotations Vonnegut uses in the first chapter become relevant. The first is from Theodore Roethke's "The Waking:"

> I wake to sleep, and take my waking slow.
> I feel my fate in what I cannot fear.
> I learn by going where I have to go. (p. 18)

The sleep he wakes to is surely death, which, along with the pains of life, is what he cannot fear and also the event toward which he has to go. The other two quotations express, first, the view that life is a dance with death, and second, the wish to stop the action of life so that it will not come to an end. What these quotations seem to add up to is the view that life is "a duty dance with death," an inevitable course leading to an inevitable end. To fear either life or death, to be immobilized by fright or horror or grief, means to give up living and become a pillar of salt.

We might conclude from this that Vonnegut advocates acceptance of the unchangeable course of life and of death itself, not looking back, enjoying the dance and the good moments life brings. As he says, "People aren't supposed to look back" (p. 19). But they do, and that they do is human and lovable. That undercuts the apparent assertion about the way life should be lived, as does the fact that it so closely resembles the system, derisively portrayed, by which the Tralfamadorians shut their eyes to the bad moments and travel in the times of happiness. Vonnegut speaks in the final chapter of being glad to have so many nice moments in his life, but there are not many offered in *Slaughterhouse-Five*. The one he mentions, of flying over East Germany in a Hungarian airplane, is punctuated with thoughts of bombings and the world's overpopulation, and set between accounts of political assassinations, Vietnam death tolls and Dresden corpse mines. As the novel ends, Billy is enjoying a happier moment in springtime sunshine, but the coffin-shaped wagon stands nearby and the bird overhead repeats the questioning *"Poo-tee-weet?"* The ambiguities persist to the end.

In general terms, however, the advocacy of keeping going, avoiding becoming unstuck in time through obsession with the painful past, and making the most of the happy moments, seems to be endorsed through the presentation of the British POWs. They are also undercut: the error which gives them five hundred Red Cross parcels a month instead of fifty detracts from the notion that they have succeeded entirely by their own efforts, and the German commandant's anglophiliac admiration of them adds to the touch of parody in their description. Yet the tribute paid them in the novel seems as genuinely intended as the criticism of the American prisoners, and the merits of their approach in contrast to that of their allies stand. For five years they have kept going in circumstances which, parcels or no parcels, remain demoralizing, and, more than that, they have given meaning and purpose to an existence as absurd as any imaginable. Perhaps through them we are shown the value of giving life purpose and making happiness rather than constantly turning away to ask, "Why me?" "Do I feel happy?" or "What does life mean?" Their system works better than anything else we see in the novel. And yet, finally, we are left feeling it does not really carry much weight. Vonnegut stops well short

201

of offering us a program for life, as if afraid that if he does he, too, might be guilty of giving us a set of lies which make life tolerable. In fact, there is far less affirmation in this novel than in *The Sirens of Titan*. There are indications of values placed on compassion, uncritical love and the joy of living, but they seem pallid and weak in this context of nightmare. We are left with the stillness following the disaster, the vague promise of that tired, faded spring light, and the bird's eternal *"Poo-tee-weet?"*

Yet *Slaughterhouse-Five* is not a humorless book. It has its full measure of the usual delightful satiric barbs, slapstick scenes and comic preposterousness. The account of the drunk Billy searching desperately for the steering wheel of his car not knowing that he is in the back seat evokes laughter but seems like something we have seen before (pp. 40-1). Billy's coming unstuck in time while watching television, so that he sees a war film backwards then forwards is funny, satirically sharp, and thematically to the point. But much of the humor remains dark or even embittered. Typical is the repetition of the Tralfamadorian "So it goes" after each mention of death. The repeated phrase becomes something like an incremental refrain, building meaning with each restatement. At first it seems funny in an ironic way, then it begins to sound irritating, almost irreverent. Gradually we realize that our irritation is right, that the punctuating refrain is forcing us to look at another then another death, and we are won over to the device, our resentment now directed to the fact which it emphasizes, that too many people are killed. "So it goes," initially almost a shrugging acceptance of the inevitable, becomes a grim reminder meaning almost the opposite of what it says, and finally another more poignant kind of expression of the inevitable. By the last chapter, when it is applied to the deaths of Robert Kennedy, Martin Luther King, and young men in Vietnam, the device which had first brought smiles leaves us close to tears. And so it goes.

In the first chapter, Vonnegut calls *Slaughterhouse-Five* a failure. We can understand why he might think so, since it is so evidently an attempt to capture the full measure of such a personally significant event and perhaps even a great deal of what he believes about life in general. Few men are likely to finish such an effort feeling they have said it all or said it right. He might also feel that technically the novel has inadequacies. It does. Some of them, such as in characterization, have been mentioned. Yet overall *Slaughterhouse-Five* remains a remarkably successful novel, and in some ways Vonnegut's best. It shows less of the warm humanity which we come to feel is part of Vonnegut's vision of life than we might hope for and than we find in *The Sirens of Titan*. It also finds less to affirm, too. But *Slaughterhouse-Five* is an enormously truthful book, and truth in this case leaves little room for faith or assurance that is the least bit forced. The novel flirts with the dangers of being episodic, disjointed, too diverse, and even too brief, for its content. In this respect it is a daring novel, but that artistic recklessness pays off. The structure does hold, and succeeds in pulling together not just its own components but ideas and themes from previous novels. And all without turning the book into a compendium. The compression gives a story which could become turgid vitality, yet at the same time intensifies its poignancy. Moreover, the novel neither falters from, nor sensationalizes the horrors it depicts, and tenaciously avoids pedantic or moralistic commentary; no small achievement given the subject matter and the author's personal closeness to it.

VII

The World of Kurt Vonnegut

Looking back over the six novels, we might be tempted to see them as answering more questions, explaining more of life, or rendering the world more knowable than they do. The foundations for Vonnegut's conception of our world are laid in *Player Piano*; the framework is erected in the subsequent novels; then *Slaughterhouse-Five* tops off the whole structure. Because Vonnegut consistently uses the same terms, builds on established concepts, and returns to familiar themes, images, phrases, incidents and characters, it is easy to be lulled into feeling that he presents a comprehensive vision. This is not to denigrate the breadth of vision in his novels, but to clarify its nature. Vonnegut places considerable emphasis on the fact that we know very little about a great deal. To see his novels as explaining or answering large philosophical questions would be to do them a disservice. Or, to put it another way, his explanation might be that there is much that we do not, and perhaps cannot know, and that to embrace formulae which seem to offer answers is dangerous. The novels voice numerous reminders of this warning. While they repeatedly raise questions about the nature of universal controlling forces and the meaning of life, they persistently show that although some apparent characteristics are discernible, we have no final answers. The closer the fiction moves to what, if taken seriously, might be seen as an explanation of cosmic order or the ultimate purposes of existence, the more cosmic, the more fantastic, the more undercut the vision becomes, and instead of a divinity we see clockwork tangerines from Tralfamadore or animated plumber's friends. Again and again the novels stress that we do not know, from Billy Pilgrim's "tremendous wang . . . You never know who'll get one—" (*Slaughterhouse-Five* p. 115), to the riddle of what controls the Tralfamadorians who control the Earthlings in *The Sirens of Titan*. In *Cat's Cradle* and elsewhere comes the warning that religions, politics, psychologies or fictions can be no more than patterns of useful lies to answer the unanswerable. In a CBS "Sixty Minutes" interview, Vonnegut made the same point directly when asked about presenting a philosophy to the young: "You know, you can give them certain kinds of information that would make them extremely tough, you know, about what God wants and all that, so you just make up something that would tend to make people gentle. It's all made up anyway, you know, we really don't know anything about that stuff."[1] Just as it would be wrong to see Vonnegut's science fiction as a prediction of the future rather than a hyperbolic description of the present, so it would be wrong to approach Vonnegut as a philosopher with final answers to the meaning and nature of our world. In fact, his greatest service in terms of workaday philosophy may be his insistence on facing the anxieties of the inexplicable and the incongruous.

Nevertheless, Vonnegut presents a coherent description of our world, one which may not explain the grand design but which does offer some answers and assist our understanding. This vision could be loosely described as existential, in that within it existence generally precedes essence and that no identifiable meaning or purpose to existence is presumed. The workings of the cosmos remain inscrutable. Where man comes from, why he is here, where he goes to, remain unanswerables. So man continues self-consciously alone, reluctant to accept the fact of his *being* without knowing *why,* anxious to find reason, purpose and order in the universe and in his relationship to it, but seeing instead only that things happen, unpredictably, pointlessly and often cruelly. Furthermore, efforts to change what happens, to make things go in an ordered way, generally prove futile: things "just happen" anyway. To describe this, Vonnegut frequently falls back on seeming explanations which fit the conditions he depicts and which are often presented in the novels from the outside perspective of extra-terrestrial beings. Thus we see Rumfoord learning about fixed patterns of time from his chrono-synclastic infundibulum, Tralfamadorians speaking of events occurring because the moment simply is structured that way, and Bokonon saying "as it was meant to happen" of all random occurrences. Again, this is description, not explanation: the ironically advanced philosophy in each case serves primarily to emphasize the characteristics of existence as Vonnegut sees them. In short, the world according to Vonnegut appears absurd, and life within it generally seems ultimately meaningless.

Space and time travel, war, and madness become the appropriate vehicles for describing such a condition. By viewing contemporary life on Earth from a distant time or planet, or in the context of wide ranges of time and space, or through the eyes of an alien observer, Vonnegut can create at least the impression of a detached perspective on the human lot. Given the fact that human beings tend not to view their affairs with such remove, and that the outsider's perspective actually may be rather idiosyncratic, the resultant portrayal is likely to abound in preposterousness, incongruity, and irrationality. War provides the ultimate measure of man's folly, his inhumanity, his inability to match means and ends, and his incapacity to maintain an ordered control over his destiny. Few institutions provide more literal examples of the absurd than an army, and seldom are purposelessness, meaninglessness and the arbitrary workings of inscrutable forces more obviously manifest than in wartime. Madness, neurosis and eccentricity characterize, with greater and lesser exaggeration, both the irrationality of such human social behavior and how society tends to view deviant but perhaps more rational and moral individual acts. They also serve to indicate the human consequences of living in a universe and a society which men find so cryptic, purposeless and frequently adverse. Physical maladies often join with the emotional ones to emphasize the stresses such a world places on its inhabitants.

Vonnegut's rendering of this world in immediate social terms defies summary in its extensiveness. His profuse satire touches on so many aspects of modern society, and of the American scene in particular, that one hardly knows where to begin short of retelling the stories themselves. Some targets stand out as the ones selected for the most devastating and frequent attacks—the military establishment, big business, capitalism generally, war, automation, politics, nationalism—while others are treated repeatedly but with more mixed feelings—man's search for an answer outside of himself, art, sex, religion, even the shocks of childhood and the pains of old age. Of course, satire is not the only mode for Vonnegut's extensive social commentary. Sometimes his intent seems to be simply the factual exposure of the often neglected, at other times he speaks with indignation of the sufferings, foibles and injustices he observes. Frequently his tone in speaking of such things is wry, like the weary humor of a man disillusioned but still able to chuckle and say, "So it goes." Certain settings recur—Ilium, the suburban township, the Rumfoord estate, Indianapolis, and, oddly, the Carlsbad

207

Caverns—until they become recognizable emblems of their respective features of American life. There are also frequent references to public figures—Barry Goldwater, the Kennedys, Roy Cohn, Martin Luther King—and to topical events. The effect is to create a literary world which comments broadly on the real world. This fictional setting gains significance and verisimilitude by its contemporary social allusions, so that even its fantasy affects reality, while its contemporaneity is set in the context of history (historical references are frequent in Vonnegut) and of the timeless patterns of human behavior.

Within this setting we find the inhabitants generally sharing enough characteristics to suggest what Vonnegut sees as the norm of contemporary man's response to his condition. Puzzlement appears widespread. Men ask, "Why me?" of the faceless forces which shape their lives, and wonder "What are people for?" Even those like Senator Lister Rosewater, who possess religious conviction or some other purposive view of existence, wonder why things do not at least run more smoothly. Whatever powers there be move in rather too mysterious ways, their wonders to perform—leaving most men troubled. This condition breeds anxiety, which the majority of Vonnegut's characters busily try to smoke, drink, fornicate, daydream, fantasize or psychosomaticize away. Anxiety stimulates the two reactions seen everywhere among Vonnegut's people: neurosis and nostalgia. Both are consequences of anxiety, and simultaneously attempts to avoid it. When the consciousness reaches the point of being unable to endure the pains of an unalterable condition, it simply bolts down an "oubliette" away from reality into a world of illusion. Sylvia Rosewater's "samaratrophia" is a classic example, Billy Pilgrim's coming "unstuck in time" might be an extreme one, Howard Campbell's "nation for two" a more mild and typical form. The widespread nostalgia in the novels seems to arise from the pervasive feeing that things are bad and likely to get worse, so that the past appears inviting. Partly because there are no escapes within the bounds of normalcy in the real world of the present, Vonnegut's characters frequently talk and act as though they were prisoners. Their being subject to incomprehensible forces in general, and to a social and economic structure which appears overbearing and unresponsive, also contributes to their sense of imprisonment. Cells, small rooms, oubliettes, fences and prisons abound in the novels, underlining the air of confinement. And besides feeling himself a prisoner, this version of contemporary man tends to see himself as being used. He may simply believe that the economic system or a particular industry exploits him. Often the feeling is more general and vague: the inexorable Powers of which he asks "why me?" shuffle him around like a piece in some cosmic game, as if he serves some larger pattern always incomprehensible to him. The literal exploitations of characters, as by army, industry or government, frequently represent this larger exploitation.

There are no villains in Vonnegut's fiction. He tells us that comes as a result of his studies in anthropology at the University of Chicago. Perhaps so. There are no heroes either. That, too, may be the result of Chicago's "teaching that there was absolutely no difference between anybody" (*Slaughterhouse-Five*, p. 7). But the lack of real villains and heroes seems an almost inevitable consequence of the vision of the world Vonnegut creates. It is hard to conceive of men achieving true heroic or villainous stature in a world where they are so nearly pawns, so little in control of their destinies and where their actions are so often subject to chance or merely "the way the moment is structured." There exists no place for "tragic flaw" in such a world, and there are no Lear-like heroic ragings against the blind indifference of this universe. That is not to say that Vonnegut's protagonists are incapable of heroism, nor that some of them, in their endurance, resistance and sacrifice may approach heroic stature as closely as the contemporary protagonist can. Nevertheless, they work their cathartic effect on us not by heroic stature, but by their ordinariness.

The typical Vonnegut protagonists are "mortal men," often in just the sense that Falstaff meant that term— "food for powder, food for powder." Most are enduring

209

victims in some sense, while several are sacrificed to lost causes for reasons they do not understand. Their qualities are mixed, self-interest vying with idealism (as in Proteus), or cynicism with altruism (Bokonon and Jonah). In at least one, motivations, actions and the relationships between them are all ambiguous. That one is Howard Campbell, but much the same could be said of the benign Eliot Rosewater. Malachi Constant emerges as one of the "best" protagonists, but begins as perhaps the most disreputable, undertaking the journey which brings him to goodness from ulterior motives. Like many of the other characters, the protagonists feel their full share of anxiety, neurosis, nostalgia and entrapment. Some, like Constant, are distinguished by their resistance to adversity, injustice and meaninglessness. Others, like Pilgrim, remain essentially passive victims. Several of them, notably Eliot Rosewater and Billy Pilgrim, are portrayed with explicitly Christ-like characteristics, and resemblances to the Christ-figure can be traced in all of them. These resemblances are appropriate in that most of the protagonists come to learn about love, about compassion for their fellow men, and function to emphasize that imperative in their respective novels.

The nature of Vonnegut's subject matter and world view raises interesting questions about the form in which they are presented. There is no reason why a writer seriously concerned about the immediate problems of his society and the larger anxieties which burden men of his era should not use satire, fantasy, science fiction as his technique—or is there? Certainly Vonnegut's use of techniques more typical of entertainment fiction than of the kind of novel we have come to expect to treat serious subjects has led to questions about the soundness of intellect, the depth of thought, even the sincerity with which he approaches issues of such profundity. There are those who say that he treats profound matters shallowly, even frivolously. A frequent implication behind such charges is that he plays to an audience, loading rather superficial allusions to social issues and philosophical questions onto slick fiction, perhaps to make it look "heavy." Hopefully, the foregoing

210

chapters provide some answer to such criticisms. But a quick review of the development of Vonnegut's work might also lend perspective.

As has been observed by reviewers, *Player Piano* resembles the work of George Orwell or Aldous Huxley, at least to the extent that it indicates earnest moral intent in its satire of current social trends through their hyperbolic projection into the future. That serious intent appears to provide one of Vonnegut's starting points; another is the autobiographical element in the novel. Then other characteristics begin to emerge—nostalgia, science fiction for its own sake, and the non-satiric brands of humor. In the subsequent novels, these elements assume increasing importance. The novels continue to qualify as moral fables, and the autobiographical element, itself common in a first novel, also remains, even reemerging more directly than ever in the most recent one. With *The Sirens of Titan,* Vonnegut's use of science fiction achieves full scope, and from that point on, fantasy and his peculiar comic bent become the characteristics which dominate his work. To oversimplify grossly, Vonnegut might be seen as starting out along the course of traditional "serious" novelists, but inevitably going off in the direction of those other forms which are usually associated with "light" or popular fiction. Science fiction marks the point of departure, but then actually recedes somewhat in later work, replaced largely by travels of the mind, bendings of and deviations from reality which are sometimes surrealistic, sometimes simply in the realm of pure fantasy. But just as science fiction proves an appropriate mode for examining the technological world of *Player Piano*, fantasy serves well as a vehicle for the nightmares of *Slaughterhouse-Five*. (That is even true in one of Vonnegut's autobiographical intrusions, where he tells us that he was the prisoner who looked at Dresden and said "Oz.") The "serious intent" is never in question, even in *Cat's Cradle*, and by the time we get back to *Slaughterhouse-Five* we again sense the serious novelist at work in the midst of forms often associated with drugstore paperbacks: but by now the combination looks rather different. In *Player Piano* the popular

211

fiction techniques seem to crowd in upon the "serious" novelist, almost to threaten his intent. We have the sense of a writer who cannot quite make it in the terms he has chosen, or whose natural impulses lie in directions other than the form he has chosen: in short, whose style and intent threaten to part company. In *Slaughterhouse-Five* those techniques are controlled and worked through effectively, serving the novelist's serious intent and bringing him at last to grips with the central symbol of his experience and message, the bombing of Dresden.

Questions as to just how harmonious the relationship between the "two novelists" in Vonnegut becomes by *Slaughterhouse-Five* persist nevertheless. Vonnegut himself seems somewhat in doubt, saying that the novel is a failure, including the characteristic self-denigrating remarks, and again poking fun at his alter-ego Kilgore Trout—who is as ever consigned to pornographic book stores. But the tone of these comments seems a little less defensive, more assured and comfortable, than in the earlier novels. There Vonnegut often speaks of Trout and of science fiction writers generally as though both apologizing for and defending himself. In *Mother Night*, the writer-protagonist becomes super-PR man, propagandist, and—his greatest horror—pornographer. In *Cat's Cradle* the writer is again propagandist and deceiver, a spinner of illusions. Some of his deceptions can bring comfort, and he may be of therapeutic value, if only in evoking laughter which might prove a remedy for man's existential nausea. The narrator sums up this ambivalent, ironic view of his craft: " 'When a man becomes a writer, I think he takes on a sacred obligation to produce beauty and enlightenment and comfort at top speed" ' (*Cat's Cradle*, p. 156).

God Bless You, Mr. Rosewater contains much direct discussion of writers and their roles. Eliot Rosewater is fascinated by science fiction writers, in particular Kilgore Trout, and early in the story he attends a convention of such novelists. Eliot lauds their propensities to take both the long view of human existence and a close look at the implications of the modern technological age. He admits that they "couldn't write for sour apples," but finds that shortcoming more than compensated for by their sensitivity to important changes in the world, to the issues of "galaxies, eons, and trillions of souls yet to be born" (*God Bless You, Mr. Rosewater,* p. 18). Trout, with his 2BRO2B (a rephrasing of Hamlet's "To be or not to be") is the greatest of them all, Eliot declares, but the impecunious genius is a stock clerk in a trading stamp redemption store and cannot even attend the convention. The other writer in this novel is Arthur Garvey Ulm, a poet to whom Eliot had given ten thousand dollars back in the days when he was "sanely" running the foundation and patronizing the arts. Ulm immediately suffers a paralysis of his creative capacities. First the poet asks the patron what he should write, then produces nothing for fourteen years, finally writing an 800 page pornographic book entitled *Get With Child a Mandrake Root.* Trout tries to write honestly, remains poor, his books consigned to the back shelves of pornographic book stores. Ulm tries to write what he believes his patron will like, produces pornography, and becomes a Book-of-the-month Club selection. Through these two characters, Vonnegut manages to poke some fun at book clubs, publishers, reading audiences, writers, and perhaps his own anxieties. Trout's plots are close enough to Vonnegut's to suggest a relationship, no doubt the fictional writer representing a comic-pathetic vision of what the author fears his fate may be. In the introduction to *Welcome to the Monkey House,* after all, Vonnegut refers to his short stories as pieces written to support him while he wrote novels. The anxieties of failing to make money as a novelist (alluded to even in *Player Piano*), of writing in a form not taken seriously, may find voice here. Perhaps, too, Vonnegut is talking about such pressures on the writer as the knowledge that sex-and-violence dreadfuls sell well, or the dream of patronage which inevitably erodes freedom, or the awareness that the writer's craft and psychological manipulation of his audience so easily run close to the deceptions of the public relations man or the propagandist.

On the other hand, Trout does emerge as another kind

of "Jesus figure" at the end of *God Bless You, Mr. Rose-water*. He refers to himself as that, explaining that he had to change the image before working in the trading stamp store (*God Bless You, Mr. Rosewater*, p. 185). But it is he, primarily, who saves Eliot, and who preaches most of the gospel by which the book's main "Jesus figure" lives. Ultimately the presentation of Trout in this novel proves quite confident and assertive. In *Slaughterhouse-Five* we come back to the impoverished, neglected Trout once more. This time he is described as "a bitter man," friendless, making his living as a circulation man for the *Ilium Gazette* (*Slaughterhouse-Five*, p. 142). At one point he says, with some irony, that writing is like advertising, because in both you have to tell the truth or you get in trouble (*Slaughterhouse-Five*, p. 147). But in *Slaughterhouse-Five*, Trout's role needs less development, in one sense, since Vonnegut speaks of himself directly, especially in the opening and the conclusion of the novel. And in these passages Vonnegut describes himself in rather self-denigrating terms: "an old fart with his memories and his Pall Malls," whose book lacks real characters and is a failure written by a pillar of salt. One suspects that by the time he writes that, Vonnegut can do so fairly comfortably. The earlier, less directly personal references to writing and writers, however, suggest a certain concern with being consigned to the same category as pornography and pulp-novel writers, with having important things to say while perhaps being unable to say them well enough or in a way which will be taken seriously. Any attempt to diagnose a writer's inner feelings, intentions or fears from his fiction is obviously fraught with danger. Suffice it to say that there are times when Vonnegut seems to express uncertainties akin to those which trouble some of his reviewers, including doubts bearing on style and technique in relation to purpose and content.

The literary critics who appear on the radio talk show before Billy Pilgrim in *Slaughterhouse-Five* are asked to describe the function of the novel in modern society. One says, " 'To provide touches of color in rooms with all-white walls.' " The second says, " 'To describe blow-jobs artistically.'" And the third, "'To teach wives of junior executives what to buy next and how to act in a French restaurant'" (*Slaughterhouse-Five*, p. 178). Therapy, pornography and public relations again. And again that ambiguous irony in Vonnegut, spoofing in all directions but nevertheless suggesting some regret over the passing of the traditional "serious" novel. As one of the critics says, "people couldn't read well enough anymore to turn print into exciting situations in their skulls . . ." (*Slaughterhouse-Five*, p. 178). That may be in part what Vonnegut's technique is designed to counter. At least, his style does draw from the techniques of forms other than the classical novel. It resembles the television drama in its swift pace, its darting topicality, its frequent use of stock minor characters, its violence, and its use of montage effects. Like the cartoon strip, Vonnegut's fiction uses recurring characters and locales, placing an emphasis on action in a fast moving sequence of static scenes. The science fiction element provides its traditional outsider's perspective of current social norms, and offers the excitement of the future and the improbable while grounded firmly in the present and the probable, affording at once escape from and confrontation of its own peculiar vision of reality. Yet behind all these techniques which give Vonnegut the stamp of modernity lie many of the assumptions traditionally associated with the best and most representative American novels. Leslie Fiedler speaks of Vonnegut's recourse to "the first and most authentic variety of American Pop," the "quest of the absolute wilderness . . ." as found in the Western.[2] Certainly Vonnegut's protagonists, in common with their most illustrious forebears, "light out for the territory," become involved in highly symbolic journeys, confronting the wilderness of the new frontier of space. Like the Hucks and Ishmaels and Nicks before them, Vonnegut's heroes encounter existence in the broadest terms. For all the social satire and topicality in the novels, they are not like those traditional British novels

---

[2]Leslie Fiedler, "The Divine Stupidity of Kurt Vonnegut," *Esquire* (September 1970), 196.

where the emphasis falls upon the hero's relationship to his society and his finding a place within it. Rather, Vonnegut's heroes confront the universe itself, question its meaning and, in turn, their own meaning. Consequently they tend to emerge as larger than life sized, for all their being bumbling, unconfident, unheroic figures. The magnified hero, struggling with self in a symbolically cosmic wilderness is also, of course, central to the great tradition in the American novel.

Vonnegut's humor stands firmly in the American tradition, too, even though much of it is contemporary social satire particularly fitted to the tenor of the times. Again, contrast with the British tradition helps highlight Vonnegut's place in his national literary heritage. British comic fiction in the twentieth century certainly has its dark side. James Hall coins the appropriate term "painful comedy" for this form in his study of the modern British comic novel, *The Tragic Comedians*.[3] As Hall points out, the British writers balance the pessimistic aspects of their views with an assurance that "the horrors can be handled," that people will, as in former generations, find a way to muddle through. Things are unquestionably rough, but they are not hopeless. The very fact that these British novelists can treat the pains of twentieth century existence in comic terms, can see the humorous implicit in the existential absurd, in itself implies a degree of confidence. American humor tends to be short on such assurance, implying if not hopelessness then a great deal of pessimism. From Twain to Faulkner to Malamud, the comic stance is one of watching human folly not with the lively involved delight which has marked British comedy from Chaucer to Cary, but with an amused ironic detachment. This does not mean that the American humorist is unfeeling, or that he does not express a compassionate concern for the human condition. But there is a characteristic difference in the tone of his comic response. In *Cat's Cradle*, laughter is spoken of as a remedy—"if laughter

---

[3] James Hall, *The Tragic Comedians* (Bloomington, 1963), p. 5.

can be said to remedy anything." That seems to set the tone of Vonnegut's comedy, and of so much American fiction. It is done with the sense of laughing at essentially hopeless situations, of finding a joke in the way the world is going to hell (as literally occurs in Jonah's Bokononism in *Cat's Cradle*). Much of Vonnegut's humor appears to be predicated on pessimism: the joke of a man's pride in how well he designed a machine to replace himself, the grim humor of a frozen POW trying to don a coat ten sizes too small, the absurdity of a doomed Martian invasion. Behind such comedy is the vision of a society willing itself to its own inevitable destruction, of man as a hapless pawn in an arbitrary and incomprehensible world. Vonnegut admits to a pessimistic view of the world: "I can see maybe forty years' more hope."[4] He also sees himself as a "funny" writer—which he is. But what he presents as funny is often the irrational inhumanity of man and the crazy meaninglessness of the universe. That is why much of his comedy acts not as comic relief (although some of his more slapstick and folksy humor does), but as a poignant intensification of the tone of pain, weariness and subdued indignation which permeates his work.

In sum, Vonnegut can be viewed as putting the traditional American novel in contemporary dress. How successfully he does so remains the crucial question. His detractors evidently feel the contemporary techniques are slick and superficial, the substance a thin caricature of the tradition. Others find the techniques revitalize old forms and make possible a return to traditions lost or observed earlier in the century. Although the wide readership Vonnegut has enjoyed in recent years demonstrates the appeal of his technique to contemporary audiences, obviously that contemporaneity could prove a limitation in the long run. Vonnegut's fiction could become something of a period piece. As such it may emerge as one of lasting interest as a portrayal of the society and the art forms of our times, of the moods and concerns of a decade, and of how this period thought about itself and saw its future.

On the other hand, the basic questions Vonnegut's novels explore are timeless, even if the form in which they are pursued remains closely tied to a period. The breadth of Vonnegut's readership may indicate that his appeal need be no more tied to one era than to one generation. It could be that as his appeal to youth as a peculiarly contemporary and relevant writer fades, his stature with older generations as a "serious" writer will grow; in fact, the indications are strong that this process has already begun. Clearly, Vonnegut is peculiarly in tune with the mood of America in recent years, and has found a style which effectively expresses that mood. He could well emerge as one of the most representative and expressive American writers of the 'sixties. As such his reputation may continue to grow in the 'seventies.

Vonnegut has declared his intention to publish no more novels.[5] He may, of course, change his mind and revert to the form after his work with the drama, but *Slaughterhouse-Five* looks like a logical conclusion to his canon of novels, whether or not it proves to be the last. In many ways it marks the end of a cycle. Throughout, the novels grow in complexity. They are always episodic, but increasingly they move toward more things happening at once, the culmination coming in the complex structure of *Slaughterhouse-Five*. The last novel is the most psychologically probing (though not providing as complete an examination of its protagonist as *The Sirens of Titan*). Above all, it is the novel in which Vonnegut confronts the Dresden experience. In doing so, he seems to bring a quest to an end. The building echoes of himself and the references to his own earlier works help to bring all that he has written to bear on this central event, as if to say, "That is what it has all been leading up to." The science fiction and the fantasy achieve their fulfillment as the appropriate means for coping with a terrifying, haunting and absurd event which emblematizes much of the human condition Vonnegut has sought to describe. *Slaughter-*

[5]Richard Todd, "The Masks of Kurt Vonnegut Jr.," *New York Times Magazine*, January 24, 1971, 19.

house-Five is also the most directly autobiographical novel, as if the autobiographical impulse evident but cloaked in the earlier novels can at last find vent as the author comes to grips with the Dresden episode. One leaves *Slaughterhouse-Five* not with the feeling that Vonnegut has said all that he has to say, but sensing that Dresden, which has kept goading him, has finally been faced, if still not resolved to his satisfaction. Those authorial interjections at the opening and close of the novel also leave the audience with the feeling that Vonnegut has at last made himself known and spoken personally to his reader before bidding farewell.

That personal note, farewell or not, remains a welcome touch. Vonnegut is an easy writer to feel affection for. Admittedly there are times when he seems a little coy or posed, but in general the personality behind the authorial voice is a pleasant one. From what he advocates and what he affirms, as well as from what he disapproves of, one senses a compassionate, gentle, troubled man. There is a touching ambivalence in what he says through his novels. On the one hand is the constant implication that men could do better, and on the other a kind of resignation, a feeling that things cannot really be expected to go better. "So it goes." Yet in spite of the haunting pessimism, there is a recurrent affirmation that life can be improved, can be lent meaning, especially through love. Nor is his advocacy of love a trite reiteration of vague current fads or a pandering to recently voguish vocabulary. Vonnegut readily exposes the limitations of naive faith in romantic love or free-flowing goodwill. Uncritical love is never easy, and Vonnegut's heroes labor long and hard learning and practicing it. But once mastered, love proves the most satisfying source of personal fulfillment his protagonists can achieve. This points the way to Vonnegut's second strongest affirmation: that the way to understanding and meaning in life lies in knowledge of ourselves rather than in seeking answers outside. Science, technology, militarism, nationalism, politics and religion all fail in their attempts to explain and control the universe, to provide the understanding and structure necessary to meaningful existence.

219

Yet Vonnegut also cautions against the wrong kind of turning inward. It should not become an escape from reality nor an evasion of our responsibilities to others. True knowledge of self and of the relationship of self to exterior reality avoids both deluding self-absorption and dogmatic faith in programmatic conceptions of existence. In avoiding those twin distortions of perception, Vonnegut argues, lies man's best hope for behaving toward his fellows with respect, compassion and understanding. That, perhaps, is what Vonnegut tries to show us when he presents no villains and no heroes, but rather men muddling through as best they can, some a little better than others as they learn to love. And that is perhaps why he appears to place considerable emphasis on the necessity of never placing ends before means, of never treating other people brutally in the name of abstract causes or personal obsession. If men could live by this creed, life might be better. When they do, he shows, they survive the blows of their incomprehensible universe with more serenity and some joy. Unfortunately, that happens all too seldom in the world Vonnegut shows, and he obviously feels that time is running short with little hope of change. That accounts for much of the despondency in his novels. Yet Vonnegut is not a joyless writer. In fact, "Joy" is one of his favorite words, and is the one which Kilgore Trout mumbles at the end of his final appearance in *God Bless You, Mr. Rosewater*. In *Slaughterhouse-Five*, Vonnegut tries hard to assert the value of holding on to the good moments in life. It is not easy: great horrors as epitomized in the Dresden fire-raid or the Robert Kennedy assassination constantly threaten to crowd them out. But however troubled and weary the voice of Vonnegut may sound, it can invariably rise to assert the good and the joyful in life, and that remains one of its most endearing qualities. There is always the affirmation of a Chrono, son of the Space-Wanderer and born to war and suppression, who lives to say, "Thank you, mother and father, for the gift of life."

Selected Bibliography

Most of what has been written about Kurt Vonnegut has been in book review form. The items listed below represent only a small proportion of the total number, and are judged to be among the most generally helpful.

Bryan, C. D. B. "Kurt Vonnegut on Target," *The New Republic* (October 8, 1966), 21-26. Discusses K.V. as satirist: skillful, lacking in anger, taking too-easy targets.

DeMott, Benjamin. "Vonnegut's Otherworldly Laughter," *Saturday Review* (May 1, 1971), 29-32, 38. Largely concerned with K.V.'s contemporary appeal to "Youthcult."

Fiedler, Leslie A. "The Divine Stupidity of Kurt Vonnegut," *Esquire* (September, 1970), 195-203. Discusses K.V.'s "Pop Art" and its place in American literary history.

Keogh, J. G., and Edward Kislaitis. *"Slaughterhouse-Five & The Future of Science Fiction,"* *Media & Methods* (January, 1971), 38-39, 48. Discusses K.V. as surrealist.

Samuels, Charles Thomas. "Age of Vonnegut," *The New Republic* (June 12, 1971), 30-32. A generally unfavorable assessment of K.V.'s novels.

Todd, Richard. "The Masks of Kurt Vonnegut Jr.," *New York Times Magazine* (January 24, 1971), 16-30. Builds around an interview with K.V.: notes his intention to write no more novels.

HERMANN

HESSE

by Edwin F. Casebeer

Throughout his long career, Nobel Prize winning author Hermann Hesse struggled heroically, in his life and works, with some of the central questions of our age.

In **Hermann Hesse,** Edwin F. Casebeer brings out Hesse's amazing breadth of subjects, situations, characters, themes, techniques, and shows the underlying unity in Hesse's major works.

(68-965) $1.50

available wherever paperbacks are sold
